B54 01

D0197938

My Itchy Dog

How to keep your dog in
prime health (and away
from the vet!)

KATE BENDIX

Rotherham MBC	
B54 017 115 5	
Askews & Holts	29-May-2017
636.7083	£8.99
SWI	

Published in the United Kingdom in 2017 by
Short Books
Unit 316, ScreenWorks
22 Highbury Grove
London
N5 2ER

10 9 8 7 6 5 4 3 2 1

Copyright © Kate Bendix 2017

The author has asserted her right under the Copyright,
Designs and Patents Act 1988 to be identified as the author of
this work. All rights reserved. No part of this publication may be
reproduced, stored in a retrieval system or transmitted in any form,
or by any means (electronic, mechanical, or otherwise) without the prior
written permission of both the copyright owners and the publisher.

A CIP catalogue record for this book is available from
the British Library.

ISBN 978-1-78072-308-2
Printed at CPI Group (UK) Ltd, Croydon, CR0 4YY

CONTENTS

Foreword

It may seem a little strange for a veterinary surgeon to write the foreword to a book that proudly states it will reveal "how to keep your dog in prime health (and away from the vet)". But I sincerely believe that if the veterinary profession did its job properly we would more or less make ourselves redundant. Of course, some of every vet's working life is spent in dealing with emergencies such as road accident cases, performing useful surgery (such as neutering), and treating serious infections. But the majority of our time is spent on trying to deal with more minor, non-life-threatening problems. These include itchy skin; smelly and waxy ears; sticky or watery eyes; fleas, ticks and worms; stiff joints and sore gums and dental disease. Exactly the problems you will find discussed in this excellent book.

In my own work as a holistic vet, I spend a great deal of my time explaining to clients the importance of a grain-free, kibble-free diet in promoting good health. I expound my views on the unnecessary use of repeated vaccination boosters; about the overuse of antibiotics and how it leads to the rise of resistant infections; and how the same will happen with repeated use of flea treatments and wormers (it's already happening in farm animals).

I suggest using natural parasite repellents; doing worm counts rather than giving routine wormers; and many other natural medicines and supplements to add to a good diet to keep pets well, rather than treat them when they are sick.

Kate Bendix has done a fantastic job in distilling such ideas and many more into an easy-to-read, practical guide to natural ways of keeping your dog healthy. I recommend it highly – even with the knowledge that if every dog owner bought a copy and put the advice within these pages into action it could put an end to the career of many vets, maybe including myself.

Richard Allport
BVetMed, VetMFHom, MRCVS
www.naturalmedicinecentre.co.uk

Introduction

Did you know that, on average, your dog will cost you £26,000 during his lifetime? But here's the real kicker. That figure does not include the cost of healthcare. And, as all pet owners can attest, nothing makes you appreciate the NHS quite like coughing up your hard-earned cash on a vet consultation with a simple blood test thrown in. That's easily £150 right there, before the cost of any treatment deemed necessary by the result.

I know it's unseemly to drink before lunch but if you get that kind of news mid-morning you'd be forgiven for giving the gin bottle the glad eye as you watch your much-longed for week in the sun disappear over the horizon.

"But Kate, I have insurance," I hear you cry, "my dog's pancreas could pack up and leave town tomorrow and I'd be covered." So do I, my sweet, but that's an emergency situation. The question is, does your insurance cover you for treating a chronic condition for life? Most won't stretch to longer than 12 months, and how are you going to pay after that?

And what about the impromptu trips to the vet for a sudden illness, a stomach problem, for instance, which doesn't in the end require treatment? If your excess is £100 or even £150, as some are, that check-up and probotic paste won't be covered either. Wouldn't it be great to be able to pare those visits down to the bare minimum?

The solution to this potential fiscal bedlam is to keep your dog healthy and to mitigate any problems she may have by treating them yourself, as much as possible. I'm not talking about a suspected broken leg, or for a moment insinuating that you bypass your vet altogether, far from it. Diabetes, cancer, heart problems: all these need the talented scrutiny of the veterinary professional.

No, what I'm suggesting is that, for the most part, it is perfectly possible for you to treat the routine issues for which your dog might visit the vet yourself, by feeding a good diet, and by administering tried and tested supplements, herbs and natural remedies.

Itchy skin; allergies; gunky eyes and ears; creaky joints; a poor immune system: all these can be managed or sorted out permanently by taking matters into your own hands.

In the same way you can take care of everyday issues such as: fleas, worms, tooth decay and gum disease (none of which are covered by insurance) for a fraction of the cost of the well-trodden, conventional path. All it takes is sound, properly researched information, some common sense and a little bit of confidence. Which is precisely what you will find within these pages. By the end of this book you will be more than capable in the ear-cleaning department; you will know that a two-day runny tummy is likely to be just that, and how to act to alleviate the problem, not just the symptom; while a skin rash will be but a minor irritation for everyone concerned.

I know this because I've been running a business based on these principles for the past eight years. Customers have turned up with their dogs in a horrible state of persistent ill health and between us we've brought them back to full strength.

One such customer, Mike, has a Jack Russell who had been visiting the vet for seven years with a chronic skin problem. One month on a new herbal treat we have developed and she's cured. That's not too strong a word – she has both her fur and her va-va-voom back!

Lisa adopted Staffordshire Bull Terrier Molly two years ago. She's spent thousands of pounds on vet treatments for dermatitis, yeast problems and allergic reactions, which haven't worked. Molly was still bald, her ears were bunged up and stinky and she was putting on weight as a side effect of the drugs she was on. We changed her diet, and got her on a decent shampoo and some temporary supplements. It took six weeks but she's a changed dog, and so much happier.

I guarantee you that by reading this book and following the advice and tips within it you can keep your dog healthy for the majority of the time, and save yourself money into the bargain. You will also stave off the long-term, chronic diseases of later life. Here's to that.

CHAPTER 1

SKIN

So, here we are. We've landed at my favourite subject – it's the reason I started www.myitchydog.co.uk – itchy skin.

As with humans, skin is the dog's largest organ. It's a marvellous, sophisticated piece of kit: it grows hair, feeds parasites and has a nice natural covering of a yeast called *Candida albicans*, which peacefully cohabits until something sets it off (see p.15). However, unlike humans who can sweat all over – as anyone stuck on the Tube or a train on a hot day can attest – dogs can only sweat through the pads of their paws and the nose. Dogs do pant to release heat and cool down, but that's not the same as sweating. So a dog's skin, unencumbered by sweat, holds onto stuff – dirt, dander and the like – making it a feeding and breeding ground for all sorts of parasites.

A dog's skin is the gift that keeps on giving, to a critter.

Visits to the vet

In the top ten hit parade of reasons your dog visits the vet, skin problems come in at number two, after ear infections. However, when you factor in pyoderma (hot spots/bacterial infection) at number four and benign skin tumours just making the list at number nine, frankly, I think it deserves the top spot.

Itching, flaking, dry skin; weeping, suppurating wounds; and musty, yeasty, greasy skin are notoriously difficult to treat effectively because they are the symptom, never the reason for the current eruption on your dog's backside. Initially, your vet will look at treating a skin problem with steroids, which suppress the symptom – the itching, weeping, flaking – but rarely treat the cause. He or she may prescribe antibiotics (just in case there is an infection), offer strong flea treatments, and maybe even suggest changing to an expensive prescription foodstuff that no one is sure your dog needs, but let's try it anyway. All of which make skin problems a sore subject. Your dog is still chewing her paws, the pads are getting redder by the day, you're almost bankrupt with it all and yet you're no nearer to a solution.

Let me explain

In this chapter, I will take you through the most common reasons for skin problems in dogs. Once we've got it down to bite-sized chunks, this massive subject should be far easier to deal with. Not only that, but there are some incredibly good natural products out there for treating skin problems, and some simple tricks to prevent them happening in the first place.

The time of year really matters when it comes to itching in dogs. When I tell you that I sell far fewer products for itchy skin in winter, but sales take off like a rocket the minute the sun comes out and the trees begin to blossom, most of you will nod your heads sagely as you mash yet another antihistamine into your dog's breakfast. A certain amount of itching and scratching is normal in any dog. It's when scratching or paw chewing becomes constant and obsessive that you know something's not right. There is plenty you can do to minimise itching and scratching, so take heart – all is far from lost. Here are the main reasons your dog itches and scratches:

- **Canine atopic dermatitis** Also called atopy, this is often set off by an allergy to something like mites or a food stuff or something your dog's inhaled such as pollen from trees, flowers, grasses or plants, or mould spores.
- **Fungus** An overgrowth of *Candida albicans* on the skin, or malassezia, a very itchy fungal infection.
- **Household chemicals** Cleaning and laundry products can affect dogs too.
- **Grooming products** The cheaper shampoos especially can cause problems.

- **Air fresheners**[1] Research shows that air fresheners can cause neurological problems, including depression, as well as upset tummies and skin allergies in babies and dogs because they're much closer to the ground than we are. The plug-in, automatic sprays are the worst offenders.
- **Fleas, ticks, mites, lice and other insects** These little parasitic critters can be super-itchy, sometimes seasonal, always dementing. They will be dealt with in the next chapter.
- **Secondary infections, diet, stress and boredom** These can be culprits too.

Canine atopic dermatitis

This is a generic term used to describe a chronic (long-term), inflammatory skin condition caused by an allergic reaction, or hypersensitivity, to something in the environment. It comes second in the itchy skin stakes after parasites. Symptoms include unstoppable itching and scratching, paw chewing, constant grooming, skin nibbling, rashes, watering eyes, itchy ears and sneezing, sometimes with wheezing and coughing added for good measure.

Atopic dermatitis can be triggered by house dust mites (the most common type), flea bites, poor diet or food

1 http://www.tandfonline.com/doi/abs/10.3200/AEOH.58.10.633-641

intolerance. It can also be set off by something airborne that your dog breathes in. If it's outdoors the cause will be grass, pollen and/or mould spores (often called hay fever); if it's inside the cause may be air fresheners (see page 20 for more on this), scented candles (the cheaper they are the worse they are) and formaldehyde, a chemical given off by new furniture and plastic (for example a new television or hard flooring, especially if it's made from particleboard).

If the allergy is caused by pollen or grass, it will tend to be a seasonal problem, at its worst in spring and summer when the pollen is doing its thing, so you will really notice the change. If the culprit lives in your house your dog will be itching most of the time, and it may be even worse during the winter months when there is less ventilation and the heating is cranked up. Either way, your dog will be constantly scratching all over, possibly with runny eyes and nose.

What you can do to help

Adding a good blend of omega 3 and 6 oils to your dog's food will help mitigate the effects of hay fever and other breathed-in allergies on the skin. Lintbells' YuMEGA Itchy Dog is a great product. Wash your dog with a neem shampoo such as CSJ's Skinny Dip (for more on neem, a miracle Indian healing potion, see page 47). The concentration of neem, coupled with the antihistamine effects of sage, lemongrass and rosemary will reduce itching straight away. Avoid shampoos that contain sodium lauryl or sodium laureth sulphates – they're too harsh and will strip the helpful oils from the skin and fur. Also, a good rub-down after coming in from a walk, either with a cool, damp flannel or a wet wipe with a good pH – but no parabens or petroleum derivatives – will remove much of the dander and pollens that set the itching off.

If, like many dogs, yours is prone to skin rashes on the belly and armpits a T-shirt is a good way to protect her as it will keep the irritating pollen and grass seeds off. I'm not a fan of dogs wearing clothes, but in this instance it could be very helpful. Equafleece makes T-shirts for dogs that are great quality and wash very well. Put the T-shirt on your dog when you're out on a walk. Now he can frolic in the long grass with pals all he wants.

Fungus

A dog's gut, just like ours, is home to a multitude of microorganisms known collectively as gut flora. Think of these microorganisms as baby birds, all lined up and crying out for food. Now the loudest baby bird, tweeting for all it's worth, is *Candida albicans*, a sugar-digesting, benign yeast found naturally in the gut and on the skin. If your dog's immune system has been weakened by illness or a poor diet, *Candida* can become more invasive and harmful, spreading throughout the gut and erupting onto the skin, causing red and very itchy spots and patches – mostly in warm, wet crevices such as the armpits, ears, toes and groin – the result is intense itching and scratching.

What you can do to help

Fungus gets the two-pronged attack with diet and skin treatment. The first and most important thing you need to do is cut out the cheap, over-processed carbohydrate and sugars in your dog's food. Simple sugar carbohydrates such as white rice, maize, vegetable derivatives and tapioca starch are all found in large, highly processed quantities in dog food.

Candida thrives on simple sugars, and processed dog food (dry *and* wet) breaks down into simple sugars very easily. Once you start feeding *Candida* with sugar it is like a runaway train, proliferating throughout the entire gut, releasing toxins, attacking the liver and coming alive on the skin. You can treat that bad girl with as many steroids as you like, but until you change the diet (and don't be fooled into buying expensive prescription foods from the vet they're still horrible) your dog is going to itch and scratch.

What your dog needs – and we all need – are complex carbohydrates for example, broccoli, brown rice and sweet potato. Complex carbohydrates are all good as they break down into sugar very slowly. Feed your dog a good diet, with more protein from fish and meat, as well as complex carbs (see page 76 for more on this). Add a short-term probiotic to your dog's food for a couple of weeks too – Lintbells' YuDIGEST is good (see pages 75 for more on probiotics).

Tackle the external flare-up by washing your dog in a good neem shampoo and applying a soothing neem and coconut cream – CSJ's Skinny Cream is brilliant. I used it to treat my dog Nikita when she arrived covered with a fungal skin infection called malassezia and was still getting over mange (for more on treating mange, see page 43). It cleared her skin up a treat and wasn't harsh, so didn't sting.

The one thing I will say about treating fungal problems with neem is that fungus likes a fight. The skin may well flare up once you have applied the neem and can become redder and itchier for a couple of days. But the neem always wins, so don't panic or give up. Keep on with it and you'll win the battle – and the war.

Household chemicals

Skin problems caused by household chemicals often present themselves as a contact allergy that affects the parts of a dog that touch the floor: paw pads, bellies, groins and armpits, mostly. However, breathing in household chemicals can also cause issues. If you've got a dog who's really sensitive to household products, there is plenty you can do to help. Some of it sounds a bit drastic, but you can make the changes over time, as and when things need replacing – think of it as part spring-clean, part clear-out.

Vacuum often

If you have pets you will probably already have a great vacuum cleaner to deal with the onslaught of pet hair – Vax, Miele and Dyson work really well. Many of my customers also rate the Gtech AirRam, which is cordless to boot.

Do not use carpet fresheners – just vacuum the floors. If you can, wash the carpets once in a while, preferably with a shampoo for allergy sufferers. It doesn't have to cost a bomb – I picked up a second-hand Vax carpet cleaner on eBay recently.

Steam-clean the floors

If you have wooden or laminate flooring, a floor steamer is going to be your new best friend. It's like a steam iron and a mop combined. The beauty of it is you don't need any cleaning products as the high temperature of the steam eliminates all allergens.

You can also use steam cleaners on carpets. I love

my Karcher floor steamer, because I live in a high limes-
cale area and it can be descaled.

Declutter

You need to take a twirl around your house for possible
indoor culprits. Bin all your air fresheners – you don't
need them. Stay away from cheap scented candles, wash
your dog's bedding in non-bio washing powder and
don't use fabric softener – that stuff is the worst. Lastly,
keep your house well ventilated and wean yourself off all
fabric and carpet 'fresheners'. The perfumes and volatile
organic compounds (VOCs) in paints, hobby glues and
DIY products can also cause serious skin and respiratory
problems in children as well as pets. If possible store
them outside the house.

Localised washing

As for your poor dog's sore bits, there is a shampoo bar
made by Ekoneem that's so gentle and has so few ingredients it won't even sting your dog's tender paws. Also,
as it's a bar, you can target the areas in need by rubbing
it directly onto pre-wetted skin and fur. It's genius for
reducing inflammation and getting rid of the itch.

Protect your dog's feet

If the allergy becomes really bad, there is a company called Pawz that makes little socks from rubber, so fine they resemble deflated balloons. You can buy them from any good pet shop, or online. These 'socks' come in various sizes and offer protection from chemicals, and as an added bonus, they're super-grippy so great for slippery floors. So much so that I've heard owners raving about them, saying their dogs are now happy to walk on floors they were previously scared to venture onto as they no longer slip and slide about.

Air fresheners

In a recent study on the toxic effects of air freshener emissions, scientists wanted to test whether or not commercial air fresheners affected mammals. The short answer is yes. The results showed that in fact, instead of clearing the air of pollutants, they added to them. Further studies have shown that mammals who are at home a lot – pregnant women, new mothers, babies and pets – suffer more depression, wheezing, diarrhoea and skin problems as a result of breathing in VOCs contained in air fresheners. They have been linked to sick-building syndrome and sleep disturbances, too.

Grooming products

Whether you're buying shampoos and spritzes to groom your own dog or you happily hand your Cavalier King Charles over to the groomer on a Saturday morning to be washed, dried, clipped and snipped while you treat yourself to the papers and breakfast out, it matters not. A good groomer will use the product you specify, and any dog with sensitive skin needs to be washed with a gentle shampoo that won't aggravate it.

There are some excellent skin products out there for sensitive dogs these days, and you definitely get what you pay for.

Read the label carefully – look for products free from sodium lauryl and laureth sulphates, petroleum, phthalates, parabens and listed fragrances. (If you see a fragrance listed by name – limonene, for instance – it's because it has been shown to cause irritation in some users, so avoid!)

As a rule of thumb, especially when buying online, if the ingredients aren't listed in the description, shop elsewhere. The same goes for other grooming products, including wet wipes. Shampoos such as CSJ's Skinny Dip, Ekoneem and Pet Head are all great products.

Grooming product dos and don'ts

Ingredients to avoid:
- Sodium lauryl sulphate
- Sodium laureth sulphate
- Parabens
- Phthalates
- Limonene and any other fragrance listed separately

Ingredients to embrace:
- Oats or oatmeal – they're not just for flapjacks
- Coconut is very soothing
- Neem is a natural insect repellent, antifungal, antibacterial
- Essential oils such as sage and rosemary
- Glycerine, a simple product that binds the ingredients together

Secondary infections

It's hard enough getting children to stop scratching when they're super-itchy – if they have chicken pox, for instance. But it's nigh on impossible to get a dog to quit and no one wants to have to resort to the 'cone of shame' to stop it. That said, if your dog is scratching with dirty claws, nibbling and licking broken skin or rubbing her itchy parts across the carpet, she is likely as not to end up with a secondary bacterial skin infection. Luckily it is easy to treat small areas of secondary infection, and just as easy to avoid getting one in the first place by controlling the initial itching problem.

What you can do to help

The key here is not to let the scratching get out of control to such an extent that only a trip to the vet and a course of antibiotics will clear it up. Ekoneem do an organic neem oil that is great for sorting out all but the most prolific of skin infections. Apply directly to the infected area twice a day. If the infection covers a larger area, wash your dog with a good neem shampoo – choose one that has neem listed as the very first ingredient, followed by essential oils that reduce inflammation (sage and rosemary oils are great). CSJ's Skinny Shampoo is a good product. Then apply the neem oil to the worst parts a couple of times a day until it's sorted.

Poor diet

As I have mentioned (see section on fungus above), too many processed carbohydrates (sugars) in your dog's diet can lead to an overgrowth of *Candida albicans*, the naturally occurring yeast that lives in the gut and on skin. Move your dog over to a better food, possibly one that's grain-free. Do the same for treats too. And add a probiotic such as YuDIGEST from Lintbells, plus Dorwest Tree Barks powder for a couple of weeks, as this will soothe the gut. (See Chapter 4 for more information on the effects of a bad diet.)

Stress or boredom

Stress, especially around big events, can be a short-term problem that causes dogs to scratch more. Boredom, too, for example if dogs are left home alone for prolonged periods (especially in breeds prone to separation anxiety), can result in scratching.

How to prevent boredom

Interactive dog toys and puzzles are great, especially if they make the dog work out a problem in order to get food. Try www.nina-ottosson.com for the best interactive toys on the market or try a Kong, a very hard cone-shaped rubber toy that comes in various sizes and colours. These toys have a hole in them into which you can put food or treats for the dog to work at retrieving. Make your dog work for his breakfast. Stuff a toy with his breakfast the day before, then freeze it.

Giving your dog a frozen Kong for breakfast or a food-filled interactive toy as you leave for work will not only keep him entertained for a couple of hours, but also teach him to associate you leaving the house with food arriving.

How to reduce stress

Try Dorwest Scullcap and Valerian tablets, especially during events such as fireworks night, before travelling or when you have lots of guests over at Christmas, for instance.

Also, dead simple: leave a radio playing quietly near to where your dog spends most of his day. I also like plug-in diffusers that release relaxing pheromones such as Adaptil's Dog Appeasing Pheromone (DAP) or Natural Pet Remedy; you can't smell them, but they work a treat on dogs. If you think your dog's scratching is due to being left alone for long periods, you need to try and sort that out. If you can't arrange to be at home more, invest in a good dog walker.

Other reasons for skin problems

There are several breeds that are particularly susceptible to skin problems. Pale dogs with white fur (for example West Highland Whites, Dalmatians, English Bulldogs and Bull Terriers) and dogs with folds of skin such as French Bulldogs, Shih-tzus, Boston Terriers. Don't forget the long, floppy-eared brigade like Spaniels, Beagles, Basset Hounds and Retrievers, too. This lot love the water, and wet, warm ears are the perfect breeding ground for fungal problems.

Skin problems are a symptom of some rare autoimmune diseases, including Cushing's disease, an adrenal gland disorder; hyperthyroidism, or overactive thyroid gland; lupus, a condition in which the body's immune system attacks healthy tissue; and pemphigus, which is a 'catch-all' name for an autoimmune problem that mainly attacks the skin, resulting in crusting, ulcers and cysts.

Tips for a healthy skin

How to avoid skin problems:
- Give your dog a calm environment
- Don't leave your dog alone all day
- Brush your dog regularly
- Feed him the best food you can
- Keep on top of fleas and worms
- Clean and vacuum your home regularly
- Use a good-quality shampoo to wash your dog
- Invest in a DAP or Pet Remedy pheromone diffuser

Useful remedies for skin conditions:
- Pure organic neem oil such as Ekoneem
- A neem-based shampoo containing essential oils such as sage and rosemary
- Ekoneem shampoo bar
- Neem and coconut cream
- Dermacton
- DAP or Pet Remedy pheromone diffusers

Supplements that help skin conditions:
- A good omega 3, 6 and 9 fish and plant oil (eg Lintbells' YuMEGA)
- Echinacea
- Coconut oil
- Probiotics
- Dorwest Tree Barks Powder
- Herbal flea, tick and mite mix
- Herbal wormer

Skin problem checklist

Like many diseases that present with 'flu-like symptoms' in humans, a dog's skin can be itchy for all sorts of reasons. One or many things could be going on at once. Have a chat with your vet to make sure there's nothing more sinister underlying the itching, then you can get on with treating it as naturally as possible. It may never go away – it may be a case of just managing the problem. Remember that the symptoms are the immune system's way of responding to something it sees as an invader. Long-term steroids will only mask the problem, and long-term antibiotics will weaken the immune system further. See if any of the symptoms listed below can give you a clue to what ails your dog.

Symptom	Possible cause
Itching at the base of the tail and down the back	Fleas, worms or blocked anal glands
Chewing at the top of back legs	Blocked anal glands, worms or fleas or a reaction to whatever your dog has been rubbing against, trees maybe
Chewing and licking paws constantly, often resulting in brown staining of the fur	House dust mites, harvest mites, grass seeds or *Candida* overgrowth
Itchy, red and sore belly, groin and armpits	Bites, contact allergy to grass, sarcoptic mange (see page 44)
Itchy face, especially with fur loss around the eyes	Demodectic mange (see page 44), or simply sticking their faces into plants that don't agree with them
Itchy paw pads	House dust mites, harvest mites, a sensitivity to cleaning products or *Candida* overgrowth
Itchy, gunky, smelly, red ears, with lots of head shaking	Ear mites, harvest mites or *Candida* overgrowth

Symptom	Possible cause
Circular patches of hair loss	Ringworm, which is actually a fungal condition
Little red spots on the skin	Allergy or folliculitis, a mild bacterial infection, secondary probably to another condition, such as mange
Little raised lumps under the skin	*Candida* overgrowth, *Malassezia* (more fungal loveliness) or heat rash
Itchy, runny eyes, runny nose, wheezing, sneezing or coughing	Canine atopic dermatitis, possible hay fever
Smelly skin	*Candida* overgrowth, seborrhea (they'll also have greasy, scaly skin with this one)
Hair loss, more shedding than usual	Stress, environment, central heating, poor diet
Greasy, scaly skin	Seborrhea due to allergies, hormone imbalance, or too much protein in the diet
Skin colour or texture changes	Untreated long-term skin problem or hormonal changes – talk to your vet
Itchy, raw patch on foreleg, or lick granuloma caused by excessive licking	It could actually be that your dog is in pain – talk to your vet
Red, irritated patches of raw skin, probably a hot spot	Could be allergy, bites or the result of chewing and licking that spot

CHAPTER 2

FLEAS, TICKS
and MITES

Parasites such as fleas, mites and ticks are a fact of life with dogs. Keeping on top of them is one of the key maintenance jobs you will have throughout your dog's life if you're going to keep her healthy and mischievous. After all, what's the point of dogs if they're not healthy enough to make you laugh, cry, or exasperated beyond belief?

Fleas, ticks and mites are disgusting. They suck up to our pets – taking blood, spreading disease and laying eggs. The fact that they are a different species matters not. As far as they're concerned your dog provides a source of food and a place to breed. Each one will take any chance it can to hop onto your dog, feed off the blood (or skin), so that it can develop and continue to breed. That's the way of life for a parasite. There are added extras, though – they come with diseases and even other parasites that they kindly pass on to your dog. For example: immature fleas pass on tapeworms; ticks carry Lyme disease and babesiosis; while some mites will inflict horrible skin problems. If this isn't enough, fleas, ticks and mites lay eggs by the thousand, and use your dog to make sure they're left all over the house. Fleas, ticks and mites are not a happy part of the dog world. Your job is to stop them from hopping onto your dog in the first place.

Fleas

The first thing to know is that prevention is much easier than dealing with an infestation. Most of the fleas you'll find pimping off your dog are actually cat fleas. Don't get me wrong, there are dog fleas to be found on dogs, too. But cat fleas have flatter heads than dog fleas, which makes it easier for them to move swiftly through a dog's fur – they are simply more successful and will be found in greater numbers on your dog. Fleas are opportunists; they'll jump onto any mammal if there's a free blood meal going. And if they can get a two-for-one deal by laying eggs on their host at the same time, then so much the better. All aboard! Flea infestations are seasonal and generally kick off in early spring.

So how do you know your dog's got fleas?

You'll know your dog's got fleas when you find him chewing his paws and pads and/or scratching at his groin, armpits, belly or under his chin when he lies down on the floor or in his bed. What you really need to know is that for every flea you spot on your dog there are nine more elsewhere in your house at various stages of development. What's more, you will have to treat the whole house to make sure they're all dealt with.

The flea cycle

This is how it works. A female flea lays up to 50 eggs a day on your dog. Flea eggs are white and a bit smaller than a grain of rice and are shaken off as your dog goes about his business. Eggs land on the carpet, his bed (or yours), even between the floorboards. After a few days or weeks, the larvae hatch. They move along the floor or rug, using tiny hairs on their bodies, finding food (dirt, flea faeces and dust – which as we know is mostly dead bits of human skin). Is your skin crawling yet?

When the larvae are large enough, they spin themselves into a protective cocoon or pupa while they develop into adults – just like a moth or a butterfly. And there they wait... and wait... and wait, until it's 'time'. The adult flea can stay safely tucked up inside its cocoon for months (even years) until the conditions are right for it to hatch for maximum effect; it will only emerge if it's pretty sure there's a host close by.

A flea can detect a host by vibration, changes in temperature or even a change in carbon dioxide levels as your pet breathes into the carpet. To give you an example, I bought a flat in 1999. When I moved in there was no hint of a flea. Two years later I got my two cats Pearl and Dave from the most excellent Celia Hammond Trust just down the road. Well. Within two weeks that flat was jumping with fleas. Both cats had been free and clear of worms and fleas before they came to me – I actually gave my cats fleas! Who does that? The pupae had been hiding in the carpet all this time; it was the only thing the previous owners left behind – well, that and a really skanky sofa I ditched on day one. One whiff of a furry coat was all it took to wake them up and invite them to jump aboard. Fact: flea pupae are ticking parasite time bombs.

Ticks

These have got to be the most bottom-clenching parasites of the lot. The two most common ticks found in the UK are deer or sheep ticks (in the countryside) and hedgehog ticks (more urban). But a tick is a tick; it will fall, crawl or hop onto any animal it can leech a meal off. In the garden you'll find ticks on foxes, squirrels and blackbirds as well as on the aforementioned hedgehogs.

Ticks are consummate travellers. They are tiny, self-contained and discreet and move from place to place, practically unseen. A tick might be sitting on a leaf next to a well-trodden path, minding its own business, when a dog comes snuffling about, as they are inclined to do. The tick, feeling a bit peckish, will drop onto your dog and make its way to a nice, warm and not too furry part of the body and settle down to eat. A tick won't bite immediately – it will spend time trying to find the best site. It stands on its hind legs and holds out its front pair – this is known as questing. So it's a good idea to brush your dog (and your clothes) after a walk and before going into the house.

The horror-film part

Contrary to popular belief, a tick has no head – it doesn't need one. It makes a pit in the skin, which it uses for collecting blood; the longer it stays on the skin, the deeper the pit will be. Once the tick is settled in, it releases a cement-like substance to hold itself in place, which also makes it harder to remove. Before a tick starts feeding it is tiny and very difficult to see – it can be as small as a poppy seed. But once it has fed it resembles a small bean and will be far easier to spot; it can sometimes be seen poking out through a dog's fur. A tick can suck blood for up to two days in one sitting. It begins by anaesthetising an area of skin, and then cuts into it. It inserts a barbed feeding tube (proboscis) into the hole and starts to suck the host's blood. While it is doing this it's also sucking up any disease pathogens the host may be carrying (which it will pass on to its next 'victim') or, conversely, injecting disease into its host as its saliva passes down the feeding tube. When the tick is satiated, it drops off and moves on to the next stage of its development.

Why ticks are like a pyramid scheme

As we have seen, ticks are the soul of generosity when it comes to spreading disease. Their host becomes a reservoir of bacteria from which all the other ticks in town can draw. They pass the disease on to anyone they bite – you, me, the dog or that hapless sheep over there. So one infected tick passes bacteria on to 10 other ticks. Those 10 ticks then infect 10 other animals a piece and so on. A pyramid scheme. And we all know how they end!

Lyme disease

So ticks spread disease. The most common tick-borne infection in the UK is Lyme disease (Lyme borreliosis), which is spreading quite rapidly. The Health Protection Agency (HPA) now monitors Lyme disease and since 2010 it has been a requirement of every microbiology lab to report any cases of it. Any mammal is susceptible to it, so use the information here to protect your dog, yourself and anyone you go a-wandering with. Once in the body the Lyme disease bacteria migrate to the connective tissues, spread out and eventually enter the heart, joints and brain tissue. The infection weakens the host's immune response, so the first thing you may notice is that your dog appears under the weather. The most common symptoms of Lyme disease are high fever (103°–105°F/39.4°–40.5°C), lameness, swollen joints and lymph nodes (glands), lethargy and loss of appetite. On humans there may also be a rash that is often described as looking like a bull's-eye on a dart board. The affected area of skin will be red and the edges may feel slightly raised. In humans and dogs, the symptoms may not appear for 3–30 days after being bitten.

Babesiosis

As if we didn't have enough on, there is another tick-borne disease in town – babesiosis. It is new to the UK and hails from mainland Europe. It is spread by ticks carrying the *Babesia* parasite. The trend for travelling with dogs across Europe has increased exposure to the infected ticks, and the warmer winters in the UK make it easier for infected ticks to survive the trip back. Babesiosis can be fatal to dogs very quickly, so preventing them being bitten in the first place is key to keeping it under control. Greyhounds, Staffordshire Bull Terriers and Pit Bulls – both dogs and pups – seem to be the most vulnerable, though no one's quite sure why.

If the tick that bites your dog is carrying the *Babesia* parasite it will pass it into your dog's bloodstream through its saliva. The longer the tick feeds the greater the chance of passing it on. Once in the bloodstream, it enters the red blood cells. The dog's own defences will attack the parasite, but in doing this they will actually start to destroy the blood cells too. So your dog becomes anaemic very quickly. The symptoms of babesiosis in dogs to look out for include weakness, lethargy, pale gums, red urine and fever. A serious problem is that babesiosis can be mistaken for other less dangerous diseases. The incubation period is about two weeks, but symptoms may remain mild and in some cases are not diagnosed for months or even years.

When you should call your vet

If you have found a tick or seen any bites on your dog recently and he starts to become ill, go to the vet ASAP and mention babesiosis and Lyme disease. Tell your vet where you have been walking your dog and how long ago you removed any ticks. If you have the presence of mind, keep any tick you remove, bag it and freeze it, not forgetting to put the date on the bag. That way, if your dog gets sick even after a few weeks the vet can test the tick to rule out or diagnose a tick-borne disease quickly. Neat, eh?

How to remove a tick safely

There are only two ways to do this and both are cheap and simple. Use either a fine-tipped pair of precision tweezers or an O'Tom Tick Twister. Flat-ended eyebrow tweezers are no good because they're too blunt; you want to touch the tick as little as possible. You can buy precision tweezers in craft shops or online. Many vets sell O'Tom Tick Twisters and you can also buy them online. O'Tom Tick Twisters come in sets of two, one smaller than the other, and they can be washed and reused and are recyclable. I keep a set in the house and another in the glove box of the car.

- **Using tweezers** Grab the tick with the tweezers as close to the dog's skin as possible. Pull it straight off with a smooth, but firm, movement.
- **Using an O'Tom Tick Twister** With this device you can use a twisting movement because it supports rather than grabs the tick, so there's no pressure on its mouth parts. Twisting in one direction only will free the tick's mouth parts, from the skin and loosen the cement-like saliva the tick uses to stick itself to the host. Never lever a tick with an O'Tom Tick Twister as this will result in mouth parts being left behind.

Whichever method you use, wash the affected area with soap and water after removing the tick. Then apply a little neem oil to the bite and wash your hands thoroughly.

What not to do if your dog has a tick

- Don't try to smother a tick with petroleum jelly such as Vaseline, nail polish, soap or anything else for that matter. While the tick is trying to wriggle out it can send infected blood back into the host.
- Don't try to burn off a tick, as although the body may drop off your dog, the mouth parts will be left behind and may become infected later. Also there's a risk you'll set your dog alight!
- Don't try to freeze a tick off. Again, the panicking tick will just disgorge its contents into your dog.
- Don't try to twist out a tick unless you're using an O'Tom Tick Twister. If the mouth parts break off you won't be able to retrieve them because you can't see them with the naked eye, but the area can still become infected.
- Don't ever try to pull out a tick with your fingers or a pair of ordinary tweezers; you could squeeze the body and send more of its fluids into the host.

Mites

The symptoms of a mite infestation vary quite a lot, depending on the species, but you tackle them all in more or less the same way. Each mite species has its own target audience – ears, food bins, house and so on – and they can arrive at different times of the year (for example harvest mites don't appear until July/August). They also vary in appearance and can cause anything from a minor skin irritation to a horrendous infection.

However, one thing they have in common is that they tend to thrive in warm, humid conditions – our homes and gardens, our own bodies, are perfect places. Certain types of mite can live on our skin quite happily – they don't bother us and we don't bother them. The mites that bug us the most are:

- House dust mites
- Surface mites
- Storage mites
- Ear mites
- Harvest mites
- Mange mites

House dust mites
These are tiny, opaque creatures, invisible to the naked eye. They like our homes very much, especially our

bedrooms. Mites eat our detritus, mostly our dead, shed skin. So you will find them anywhere there is dust, and if your house is anything like ordinary, there will be a lot of dust. If you're not totally grossed out already, you should know that house mites love beds, especially pillows, because the proximity to our sweaty bodies means that the humidity levels are just right. Think about that the next time you wake up drooling into your pillow.

House mites cause skin allergies, dermatitis, asthma and rhinitis in dogs, cats and humans. They account for most of the mite allergies in the UK. Symptoms in dogs are constant itching and scratching, fur loss, runny eyes and nose, and sneezing.

Surface mites

This one is nicknamed 'walking dandruff' – a great name for an over-stayer. The surface mite lives on a host for its entire life cycle of 21 days. To give it its proper name, the *Cheyletiella* mite lives on the surface of your dog's skin. As the mite feeds, it pushes flakes of surface skin around, hence its nickname. Symptoms can range from dandruff with intense itching and scratching, to hair loss, especially along the back. *Cheyletiella* is a highly contagious mite too, so if your dog has it all his playmates need treating too.

Storage mites

These are nowhere near as common as house dust mites and it's a pretty simple problem to fix. Storage mites can be present in anything that can go mouldy – grain, dry pet food, cereals, cheese – and they're a real pest for agriculture for that reason. The allergic reaction in humans is sometimes referred to as Baker's Lung or Grocer's Itch.

If your dog is itchy all the time, not just in the summer and autumn as with harvest mites, for example, then storage mites will come a close second after house dust mites as possible culprits. Look out for hair loss on the face, around the eyes, muzzle and under the chin as well as excessive sneezing, and possibly asthma.

Dry dog food doesn't come with storage mites included – they infest it only once the bag is open. The best way to keep on top of them is to either use wet dog food instead, or buy dry food in smaller amounts. When you get the bag home, store it in an airtight plastic container, and always clean this thoroughly in hot, soapy water before tipping in a new bag.

Ear mites

Ear mites are generally much more of a problem for cats, but dogs get them too. You can usually tell if your pet is being bothered by them as she will adopt the 'Yoda' pose, as I like to call it, by flattening one or both ears at a 45-degree angle to the head. However, ear mites are extremely contagious so if one dog's got them, the chances are so will any other animals she cuddles up to, and they will all need treating. An ear mite infestation is pretty easy to sort out and keep on top of – see page 102 for more information on treating ear mites.

Harvest mites

The harvest mite is in fact a member of the tick family. It's a seasonal mite and is especially pesky during the seasonal change from summer to autumn. Harvest mites can be found in woodland, long grass, parks and gardens. It's not the adult mite that does the damage – it's the larvae which swarm and feed, causing intense itching, with a digestive enzyme in their saliva. They feed for two to three days, increasing three to four times in size before dropping off. Be suspicious if you see what looks like red dust clinging to your dog's hair.

Unlike other mites, these critters like sunny, dry spots and heat. To keep harvest mites at bay, try changing to early-morning or evening walks, and avoid long grass.

Mange mites

You've probably used the term 'mangy' to describe a tatty-looking fox you've seen around and about. This is a symptom of mange mites. Domestic dogs in the UK can catch mange after coming into contact with a fox that has it. Otherwise, mange infestations tend to occur when a dog has a compromised immune system, for example because of prolonged steroid use or long-term illness. A puppy, who hasn't yet developed a mature immune system, is also at risk of catching mange from his mother. As mange mites often overtake an animal with low immunity, it's important to find out the root cause. I'd also look at nutrition and the stress levels in the environment.

If I suspected my dog had mange, I would definitely get it diagnosed by a vet because the likelihood is that it's already developed into a bacterial infection by the time I can see it. There are two types of mange mites – *Sarcoptes* mites (sarcoptic mange) burrow into the skin, while *Demodex* mites (demodectic mange) live in hair follicles:

- **Sarcoptic mange** This is highly contagious and an animal's skin can quickly become infected, too. The mite burrows through the skin, making it more susceptible to infection, and causing intense itching and crusting, especially at the elbows and in the ears. Depending on the extent of the infection, your dog may need antibiotics.
- **Demodectic mange** This type of mange isn't anything like as contagious as sarcoptic mange because the mites live at the base of hair, in the follicles, so they

are buried deep in your dog's fur. As long as your dog is healthy, these mites can live on her quite happily, just as the mites on our skin do (you really do have mites that live off your skin, believe me).

However, if the dog's immune system is overburdened, through long-term illness, for example, demodectic mange can get out of control and the mites will be visible in huge numbers under a microscope. It's thought that it's actually bacteria that cause demodectic mange – the mites prepare the ground, so to speak. Suspect it if you notice hair loss around your dog's eyes, muzzle and forelegs.

What can you do about fleas, ticks and mites?

The treatment for all these little blighters is pretty much the same. I will give a general rundown on this first, then offer more particular information on how to deal with flea bite allergies, and – absolutely crucial – how to rid your house of pests and keep it pest-free.

Start by washing the dog

A good wash with neem shampoo is vital if your dog has fleas or mites. Wash your arms with neem shampoo before you wash your dog to stop the fleas hopping onto you too. Lather up your dog and leave the shampoo on her for up to 10 minutes so that it kills both the live creatures and their eggs. Obviously you need to wash the whole dog, so make sure you use a shampoo that can be used on the face, such as CSJ Skinny Dip or the Ekoneem bar.

I had a customer who called to tell me she'd washed her dog, but missed the bit under his chin. She found fleas taking refuge there a couple of days later and had to repeat the process, including the chin this time. Rinse and dry your dog well afterwards, then chuck the towel into a hot wash immediately. You can give your dog another shampooing a couple of days later if he's still itching. In the case of fleas in particular you should comb your dog thoroughly after washing to remove any dead bugs or eggs.

Some dogs are hypersensitive to flea bites. The saliva in a flea bite irritates the skin, which can become intensely itchy. I recommend rubbing a bit of neem oil such as Ekoneem onto both flea and tick bites twice a day. This should clear them up in about 48 hours; neem's antibiotic properties will take the itch away almost at once.

In praise of neem

If you buy one product for your dog healthcare shelf, make it this wonder oil extracted from the seeds and fruit of the neem tree, *Azadirachta indica*, which is native to the Indian subcontinent. Good Lord, it's brilliant stuff. Numerous studies have confirmed the oil's efficacy. India has even won a biopiracy war against the European Patent Office over it.

The best neem oil comes from India and should be cold-pressed for maximum effect. Neem oil is antibacterial, antifungal and a powerful parasite repellent. It's even used as a contraceptive in India and Madagascar by both men and women. And, no, it's not the smell that puts lovers off. Studies show that neem, eaten in capsule form, kills sperm, but doesn't affect fertility. Its effects are reversed after a few weeks when you stop taking it.

I like Ekoneem oil because it's pure, organic and smells like cabbage on the turn. Which is what you want. If it smells lovely, be suspicious. It is the active ingredients that make it stink so if they have been synthesised out to make it more attractive to the consumer, it's not likely to be any good. I mention very specific neem products here because, as with tea tree oil, it comes in varying strengths and qualities. Neem should be organic. I will always recommend brands I trust to do the job and not harm your dog because products can be adulterated so you have no idea whether you're buying the good stuff or what is essentially axle grease.

Everyone should keep a pot of neem oil in the fridge

Use it on dogs (and cats) – a thin application is all you need. Because it's a vegetable oil and not an essential oil it's not going to do much harm if it's licked off. It's good for treating bites, burns, wounds, scratches, sore bits, dry spots and hot spots (and sweet itch in horses, too). I use it myself on mosquito bites, eczema and cuts, and it's great for nits, as my godchildren can attest. We put neem oil on the inside of our dog BB's ear flaps when they get very itchy. She sometimes scratches them until they bleed when we're not looking and if she's been on her own for a couple of hours she can do some damage. We rub a thin layer of Ekoneem onto the red sore bits, and hey presto, instant relief. I'm not kidding when I say this stuff is amazing.

How to rid your house of pests

If you've found a flea on your dog, there will be many more in the house and you need to deal with both. First things first. Gather up all the dog bedding, any other blankets he frequents and any toys that can be washed and stick the lot in the washing machine. Set it to the highest temperature items will tolerate and do a full wash, none of your eco-setting malarkey. We want those critters drowned, not just coming out needing a gentle tumble-dry and a bit of counselling.

Next you'll need to spray the house. If you have fleas in the house, you'll probably have mites too, and you need to deal with them quickly so they don't hop straight back on to the dog. To get rid of fleas fast, I would go for something like an Indorex spray, which you can get from your vet, in the first instance. It will kill adult fleas, stop their larvae and eggs in their tracks, and as an added bonus, kill off any dust mites too. Spray as per the directions and that will get you a long way towards a pest-free house.

When the spray has had time to do its stuff, you can move on to a good vacuum and steam. If you have pets, then you're probably already in possession of a decent vacuum cleaner; now is its finest hour. Break out the bag of attachments and clean everything – sofas, chairs, bed frames, bookcases, skirting boards, rugs, stairs, curtains and blinds, in between the spindles on the bannisters, in the cracks between floorboards, and all hard flooring. Leave no stone unturned.

As gadgets go, you can't beat a floor steamer for killing bugs both on hard floors and carpets. A shot of boiling steam is an ideal way of killing any remaining mites because it uses heat, not chemicals, so won't leave nasty residues on the floor to further aggravate your dog's paws.

Finally, put some of your neem shampoo in warm water and wipe down all your hard surfaces that haven't been sprayed – cupboards, etc. The neem residue will keep on working. Once you've done all that, get someone else to cook dinner while you go and have a long, hot soak in the bath. The good news now is that, having banished the infestation with some of the strong stuff, you should be able to keep on top of pest control without further recourse to pharmaceuticals. All that's required is a bit of regular attention and care.

Use a neem spray

You can buy ready-made neem spray – I recommend Skinny Spray – or make up your own, as per this little recipe. Put 5ml of cold-pressed neem oil (I recommend Ekoneem), in a plant spray bottle, with 250ml of luke-warm water, then add a drop or two of washing-up liquid to bind the water and neem. Shake vigorously (the bottle, not you, obviously). Now spray a fine mist on everything – your dog, house, decking and plants. Make sure to use it up within 24 hours as the water will start to degrade the neem after that.

Make an easy flea trap

When I posted this on my blog, I got more response than on almost anything else before or since. It works!

You'll need a shallow dish – a clean cat-food dish or a plant-pot saucer is ideal – and a plug-in nightlight. Half-fill the dish with water, add a little washing-up liquid, then swish it about with your fingers to disperse the soap. Put the dish on the floor where it can't be kicked or tipped up, but near to a plug socket; make sure it's not so close to the socket that water could be splashed into it if it does get kicked over. Plug the night light into the socket and go to bed. Fleas will be attracted to the light, jump into the dish and get wet. Soapy water is kryptonite to a flea, rendering it powerless so it drowns. In the morning you can come downstairs to count your dead fleas – you'll feel like it's Christmas and you're five again. Throw this water away and repeat nightly until you wake up one morning and discover there are no dead fleas floating about. I promise you, all this hard work will pay off in spades.

Other tips for keeping your dog and house free of parasites:

- Check your dog regularly for fleas, mites and ticks, and treat if necessary
- Brush your dog (and your clothes) before you come in from a walk in an area known to have ticks
- Keep floors free of dirt, dust and pet hair
- Vacuum the furniture and upholstery once in a while
- Wash your dog's bedding and washable toys regularly
- Bring toys in from the garden overnight to keep them away from flea- and mange-ridden foxes

---

Use a good herbal flea, tick and mite preventative treatment

As I say, we do have to keep on top of parasites. If your dog has become overrun with them, there's no doubt that a veterinary-strength pharmaceutical treatment is the way to go. Having dealt with the immediate problem, though – and despite what the four caring corporate giants that own more than 70 per cent of the parasite treatment businesses around the world will tell you – it is entirely possible to control fleas by using a simple herbal food supplement.

The best product I have found by a country mile is the aptly named Billy No Mates from CSJ. It's so good I now buy it by the pallet-load in early spring in advance of the flea season kicking off, so I don't run out. I should point out that I have no shares in this company; I just think they make really good products, and this one is made in the UK, too. Billy No Mates is basically a herbal blend of neem, lemon balm, mint, seaweed and fenugreek. If you hold the pot up to your nose you get a warm, sweet smell. What makes it so effective against fleas and mites, I hear you ask, sceptically. First, it contains neem, the key parasite repellent. Neem doesn't actually kill fleas, but it does repel them. Neem also acts on the flea's hormones, inhibiting their growth and egg-laying capabilities. Fleas will drop off an animal that is eating neem, if they latch on at all. Secondly, Billy No Mates's other ingredients promote good gut health.

The healthier the dog, the better she is at repelling fleas and mites. Seaweed contains iodine, which is good for the thyroid in small doses, and is thought to help deter worms from taking up residence. Fenugreek is a natural anti-inflammatory, while lemon balm is used in herbal medicine not only to cleanse the gastrointestinal tract, the liver and the bile ducts, but also for disorders of the central nervous system. So in addition to repelling fleas and other pests, you're helping your dog to get his internal house in order, gut-wise. Your dog will develop a very sleek and shiny coat into the bargain.

To prevent parasites becoming resistant to herbs it's a good idea to stop using these supplements when the weather gets cold, at least for a few weeks. There are far fewer fleas about the place in winter so it shouldn't be a problem. You can always spray a little neem onto bedding in the interim.

CHAPTER 3

WORMS

We all attract parasites, they're just a fact of life. Some parasites permanently live on, or in, any living thing – dogs, cats, horses and humans. There's very little we can do to avoid coming into contact with these little blighters. Their very survival depends on them being good at seeking out an affable host, then hopping on board with a minimum of fuss to feed and breed – quite simply it's their job! In the previous chapter I dealt with parasites that live on the skin. This chapter is devoted exclusively to internal parasites, worms, which by the way, are even easier for dogs to pick up than fleas. All your dog needs to do is lick a blade of grass containing worm eggs and she will be infected.

Someone told me recently that 70 per cent of pets in the UK are never wormed. According to the British Veterinary Association (BVA), scarcely any records are kept about worm infections, except for lungworm infections (which can be fatal). So the question is: do we need to worm our dogs? The short answer is yes, but not always. There are two ways you can worm your dog: 1. you can give her a chemical wormer or a herbal wormer. 2. You can go for something called worm-egg counting – see box on page 57. I bet you didn't see that coming!

Worm types

Worms come in several shapes and sizes. They enter an animal through the mouth or are passed on in blood, and in the case of puppies, via their mother's milk. The most common types of parasitic worms found in dogs in the UK are roundworms (the *Toxocara* roundworm being the most prevalent by far) and tapeworms. Roundworms are white, resemble bits of string and can grow to several centimetres in length. Tapeworms can grow to 50cm long, but release segments that look like short bits of flat linguini or grains of rice. If you think you've lost your appetite now, read on – you'll never look at pasta the same way by the time I've finished. Both tapeworms and roundworms live in the intestines and have been known to share space with a couple of other creatures: hook-worm and whipworm (though these are less commonly found in dogs in the UK). The incidence of lungworm infection, on the other hand, is on the increase, and as mentioned above, is being monitored by the BVA as it can be fatal if untreated.

Worms need your dog!

You really couldn't make the worm cycle of life up – it's like another horror film. Worm eggs in faeces, or the soil around it, need to be eaten by a dog (or cat) so that they can hatch and develop into larvae and (yet) more worms. These worms live and grow in your pet's intestines and lay millions of eggs. The new eggs are passed out in yet more faeces, to be ingested by another animal, so the whole process can start all over again. The tapeworm hangs onto the intestinal wall by its head, releasing egg-packed segments that are passed out through the faeces. These segments will wriggle for a bit before drying out.

Signs that worms are present

The chances of you actually seeing live worms wriggling in your dog's poo are slim, because a dog can be carrying around one heck of a worm burden in its gut but only be passing out the eggs in its faeces, which are invisible to the naked eye.

The one exception to this is if a dog has so many worms that his body has to get rid of them. Then they will pass out in faeces (or be coughed up, in the case of lungworm); or, if passed out in 'sections' as discussed above, they will live outside the dog's body around the anus and you may see them moving a bit before they die.

Young puppies merit a special mention here: if they have worms, they are likely to be particularly badly affected because their bodies are so small – you might see long white worms in their poo, or tape worm sections lying in long rows or clumps – which is why it is so important to worm them with a veterinary wormer from two weeks of age.

Either way, be aware that if you don't see worms wriggling free of that poo you're bagging up, it doesn't mean your dog doesn't have them. In lieu of unde-niable evidence of your dog having worms, you're looking for subtle (and some not so subtle) signs which can be some or all of the following: weight loss; dry, course fur; diarrhoea; vomiting; increased appetite; and more bottom licking than usual (as if that were possible!).

Worm-egg counting

If you don't want to treat your dog for worms just for the sake of it, go for a worm-egg count, generally known as a faecal egg count, or FEC. A sample of your dog's poo is put under the microscope to look for eggs. The FEC not only identifies worm types present; it also calculates the number of eggs found (if any) to give an indication of the overall level of infection. This way you can treat a problem that actually exists instead of simply giving

---

your dog a wormer every month for worms that may or may not be present. If you're going down this route, though, you need to be diligent and do a worm-egg count four times a year to make sure your dog is protected.

So how can you get an FEC
As I can't see *Worm-Egg Counting for Beginners* taking off, certainly not when there's Netflix, I recommend that you do your worm-egg count by post. Yep, you can send poo by post. Just order a kit from www.myitchydog. co.uk, follow the instructions, send it off and the results will come back to you from the lab via email in a few days.

Lungworm - a special mention

It's particularly important to look out for signs of this potentially fatal parasite.

Your dog can pick up lungworm from eating or licking infected slugs, snails and frogs, or from licking egg-infected snail trails on paths or grass. If a snail has been in your dog's drinking water or a supply of water in the garden – a neglected plant tray or a water feature, for example – lungworm can get in that way too. Foxes can also harbour lungworm, excreting larvae in their poo as they go, which as we all know dogs just love to roll about in. Foxes don't bury their poo, but leave it placed strategically in order to mark their territory – usually outside my back door!

'The lungworm travelator' - how it works

You know when you're heading for your departure gate at the airport and you come to that long walkway that has a moving travelator in the middle? Well, if you are a lungworm, the travelator – your path to nirvana – is the lungs. I guess that makes your dog the North Terminal at Gatwick, pushing this analogy too far perhaps, but this is serious. I tell it as a story so it sticks in your head. If your dog eats or licks a slug and ingests lungworm larvae as a result, he is now infected and the larvae have started their journey along the travelator. The larvae move to the gut where they penetrate the gut wall and enter the bloodstream, eventually reaching the right side of your dog's heart, where they become adult worms. Here, they release eggs that hatch in the blood. The newly hatched larvae then make their way to the lungs, rupturing the lung wall and entering the alveoli (the tiny air pockets in the lungs). When they reach the top of the lungs, they make the dog cough (one of the symptoms), so bringing the larvae into his throat. He then swallows the larvae and they pass through his gut to exit the body in faeces so the whole process can start all over again. And that, my friends, is how the lungworm travelator works. You're cleared for take- off, doors to automatic. Have a nice flight.

How do you prevent and treat lungworm?

Luckily for your dog, there is no known resistance to lungworm treatments yet, so she doesn't have to suffer. It's estimated that 2 to 6 per cent of dogs are healthy but infected with lungworm, making them asymptomatic carriers (or carriers with no symptoms). If you suspect your dog has lungworm take him to the vet, ASAP. You can also do a worm-egg count specifically for lungworm (see page 57) – get your kit from www.myitchydog. co.uk.

You can treat your dog for lungworm in one of two ways – conventionally (with Advocate, which treats fleas, ticks and lungworm, or Milbemax, which also treats round-, hook-, whip- and tapeworms), or herbally (with Verm-X or Four Seasons). If you want to go down the herbal route then you MUST overlap a conventional treatment with the herbal one. Simply administer a conventional lungworm treatment as normal and start on Verm-X or Four Seasons at the same time. This is because the herbal products can only eliminate any eggs or larvae that are still in the gut; it doesn't treat any parasite that has already left the gut and is elsewhere in the body. By overlapping the treatments you get rid of what's there and allow the herbal wormer to take over. After that you can just use the herbal wormer alongside regular worm-egg counting to control lungworm. I don't know about you, but that's enough about lungworm for me.

Why it's vital to worm mums and puppies

Puppies and breeding bitches definitely need worming. Breeding bitches should be wormed before and after giving birth – from day 40 of pregnancy to two days after whelping. Panacur is the only licensed wormer for this treatment in the UK. You might not think puppies need worming as they haven't ventured out yet, but the worms are right there, and mum is the culprit. Puppies need to be wormed every two weeks until they're 12 weeks old because they get roundworm via the placenta while in their mother's womb and worms can also be passed to them via their mother's milk. Ask your vet for the most up-to-date information on puppy worming guidelines. If a puppy isn't wormed it will pose a danger to children too. The Toxocara roundworm is the most common worm in puppies and it can cause blindness.

You get what you pay for

The golden rule is don't skimp on worming treatments. Buy a good one. Spend the money to make sure your dog is clear of these parasites – this rule applies to conventional as well as herbal parasite control. Get something that does what it says on the tin, either from your vet or buy what your vet recommends online. If you do a worm-egg count four times a year, you might not need to worm at all. The money you spend on parasite control will save you a fotune in vet's fees..

CHAPTER 4

DIET

The right food makes a big difference

We are what we eat. We all know that what we eat is crucial to our own long-term health. Eating a variety of foods that are as unprocessed as possible for the majority of the week goes a long way towards helping us stay slimmer and fitter, sleep better and have far more energy.

On the other hand, if we eat highly processed carbohydrates, meat products and ready meals, with not a whiff of a carrot or a decent apple in sight, the pounds will start to pile on. Just to make matters worse, we feel tired and sluggish, with achy joints added for good measure. Most people are also well aware that if they carry on eating this way they're heading for obesity and a number of chronic diseases further down the line, such as type 2 diabetes, heart disease, cancer, inflammatory bowel disease and skin problems. If you've got yourself into a middle-aged state of being overweight and feeling lethargic with aching knees (me), you'll probably also know that by changing the way you eat you can reduce your risk of many chronic, life-shortening diseases (also me). Well, you won't be surprised to hear that this all applies to dogs too.

Millions of dogs are overweight because their lives have come to mimic our own – they're overfed, under -exercised and stressed. So it stands to reason that dog health is starting to follow the same path and disease pattern as human health. Over the past 20 years, the incidence of obesity, diabetes, heart disease, cancer, inflammatory bowel disease and skin problems in our dogs has rocketed. Now compare the list of human diseases in the previous paragraph to the dog list you've just read. Do you notice any similarities? By the same token, changing what and how you feed your dog can result in dramatic improvements to his health, life expectancy and quality of life. It's even possible that he will be able to give up some long-term medications after a change of diet, though you shouldn't EVER just swap your dog's tablets for carrots without speaking to your vet first!

Top ten health improvements

If I listed all the health improvements you can expect to see from changing your pet to a better diet you'd die of boredom, so here are the top ten:

1 Weight loss
2 No more overgrowth of the yeast *Candida albicans*

(see page 15)

3 Better skin and a glossy coat
4 If a dog has diabetes, it improves as blood sugars level out
5 Clear eyes and ears that don't smell or suffer repeat infections
6 Less itchy skin from food intolerances and allergies
7 A stronger immune system so he is better able to fight off infection and illness
8 Improved gastrointestinal health, so less poo to clear up, no more constipation or blocked anal glands, no more room-clearing wind or doggie smell and sweeter breath
9 Better joints and so improved mobility 10 A fitter, happier dog with more energy

Your dog's digestive system

It helps to understand how your dog's digestion works before you embark on any dietary changes. The canine gastrointestinal tract, or gut, isn't like ours. In humans the process of digesting food starts in the mouth. As we chew food, enzymes in our saliva set to work on our food while it can still see daylight. In dog's, however food only starts to be processed once it's landed in the stomach. A dog's stomach contains hydrochloric acid, which breaks down lumps of protein and bone, turning them into a liquid before they pass into the small intestine. If the lumps are too big for the stomach to handle, a dog's strong regurgitation reflex (peristalsis), enables him to throw the food back up to be re-chewed into smaller, more manageable pieces, then re-swallowed. Grim, but handy! The high stomach acidity is also why dogs can cope with eating three-day-old pizza and not spend days wondering which end they should point at the loo first, like we would.

Once in the dog's small intestine, the nutrients in food pass through the gut walls, into the body and off to wherever they're needed. Some foods continue into the large intestine, where the last vitamins and minerals are absorbed. The rest is waste matter that is excreted and left for you to pick up, you lucky thing.

What your dog eats can show on the outside
Think of your dog's digestion as a pipeline. Food, treats, water, supplements, drugs, bits of paper, plastic and/or glitter (or whatever your dog's proclivity is for banned substances) go in one end, and waste in the form of urine and faeces comes out the other. What goes in is not only reflected in the 'state' of the waste – wind, diarrhoea or that gelatinous, bloody horror show (colitis) – but also shows up on the outside. Smelly skin, gunky eyes and ears, blocked anal glands and greasy fur are all partly a reflection of the health of your dog's gut, and changing

to the right diet can work wonders to improve things.

Variety is everything

Imagine eating beans on toast every day, week in, week out, for all of your life. Now, while I can think of nothing finer than a tin of baked beans poured over hot, buttery toast on a winter's evening, I can't imagine what physical, emotional and mental state I would be in if that's ALL I ever ate. Before you pull me up short, yes, I know that dog foods have to be what's referred to in the trade as 'complete' so dogs get all the basic nutrition they need from one source. However, that doesn't stop a dog keeling over from boredom or worse, smelling awful, farting and pooing for Team GB or becoming overweight (with all the subsequent health problems that entails). On top of that, your dog may develop an adverse reaction to, for example, chicken, simply because that's all she has ever eaten.

The key to providing a healthy diet is confidence in yourself for the most part (you can read the labels or cook a basic meal for your dog), but also in your dog, as she has taste preferences too. For instance, my dog Nikita can't stand fish, however it's presented. If you hand-feed her a piece of roasted cod, she will either reject it outright or, if she's feeling extra polite, take it from your hand, turn her back on you then drop it gently on the floor and walk away. Offer her a bit of kidney, though, and you'll be lucky to keep your fingers.

So offer variety. This can mean healthy pet food, home-cooked meals and/or raw food (see below) if your dog likes it. That way you're going to have a healthier dog who lives longer.

Don't be afraid to experiment

Importantly, make sure that whatever you give your dog is good quality, whether it's raw, wet, canned, dry or baked. With dog food, more is less. The better the ingredients that go into the food you choose for your dog, the better it will br digested - and the less you'll have to clear up.

Raw feeding

I'm not going to come over all raw-feeding militant on you now. If you fancy a trip down the raw feeding route, there is a brilliant way to start your journey (and find out whether your dog likes it) – buy it ready-made! I give Nikita Natural Instinct's raw dog food once in a while (from www.naturalinstinct.com). It contains everything your dog needs. If your dog likes it and does well on it ,you can either stick with it or, if you fancy experimenting, try The Dog's Butcher run by Joanne down in Devon (www.thedogsbutcher.weebly.com).

Raw food certainly doesn't always agree with Nikita. One batch of frozen raw food I tried her on resulted in the worst dog breath I'd ever encountered, as it was too rich for her gut. I noticed her breath when we got into the car so we drove (quickly) down to the beach with the windows fully down. The next day I changed back to her old food and she was as right as rain.

If you're going to DIY your raw feeding, the basic rule of thumb is to feed either one-third raw meat and bone (of which only 5 per cent of that should be bone), one-third cooked carbohydrates and one-third fruit and veg or 80 per cent meat and bones (again only 5 per cent bone) and 20 per cent fruit and veg. There is no need to eliminate carbohydrate from your dog's diet, just avoid wheat and soya. I would also say that a good food processor is highly desirable for making your own raw food. Look on ebay there is always someone getting rid of one, often barely used, for a fraction of the price of a new one. The meat content should be fresh meat (any) and offal, or completely thawed frozen meat (don't refreeze it). Only ever feed your dog raw bones. NEVER, EVER give her cooked bones. Fish is safe too. Broccoli, carrots, green beans, kale and sweet potatoes are good for the vegetable part.

Home-cooked food
Changing over to raw food can help, but it's not the

only answer. If you fancy cooking for your dog, use the rule of thirds again and make her meals one-third lean protein, one-third good unprocessed carbohydrate, one-third fresh vegetables and some fruit. The chart below provides a list of ingredients that are safe for dogs and gives an idea of the vitamins and minerals that should feature in your dog's diet and why.

Food	Vitamins and minerals	Benefits
Lean meat and fish – I would probably avoid beef as it can be associated with intolerances (see Chapter 5)	Vitamins – thiamin (B1), riboflavin (B2), niacin (B3), B6 and B12	Good source of protein, which builds and repairs tissue – hair and nails are mostly made of protein. Build bones, muscles and cartilage.
Green, leafy vegetables, asparagus, cauliflower, courgette, cucumber, corn (off the cob), celery, peppers	Vitamins – A, folate, C, K Minerals – iron, calcium	Good for heart health, bones, kidney function and immunity.
Seaweed	Vitamins – A, B (especially B12), C Minerals – calcium, iodine, potassium, magnesium	Good for nails and coat condition. Kills bacteria that cause plaque and tartar build-up on teeth.

Food	Vitamins and minerals	Benefits
Apples	Vitamin C	Good source of fibre (good for digestion and can help with diarrhoea). Vitamin C helps maintain the immune system.
Bananas	Vitamins – B6, C Minerals – manganese, copper, potassium	Good source of fibre (good for digestion and can help with diarrhoea). Potassium is good for maintaining proper heart function and regulating blood pressure.
Watermelon (seeds removed)	Vitamins – thiamin, riboflavin, niacin, pantothenic acid, B6 and folate Minerals – magnesium, phosphorus, potassium, zinc, copper, manganese, selenium, choline	Helps coat condition and eye health. Watermelon also contains the pigment lycopene, which some studies suggest benefits asthma sufferers.
Strawberries	Vitamin C Minerals – manganese, potassium Also contains the antioxidant polyphenol	Excellent source of vitamin C, which boosts the immune system, lowers cholesterol and is good for eye health.
Blueberries	Vitamins – C, K Mineral – manganese	Good source of fibre (good for digestion and can help with diarrhoea). Boosts the immune system.

Food	Vitamins and minerals	Benefits
Cranberries	Vitamins – pantothenic acid, C, E, K Mineral – manganese	Help prevent urinary tract infections (UTIs), good for immune system, good anti-inflammatory. Source of fibre (good for digestion and can help with diarrhoea).
Raspberries	Vitamin – pantothenic acid, biotin (B7), folate, C, E, K Minerals – manganese, magnesium, potassium. Also contains omega 3 fatty acids	Good for bone strength, kidney function and immunity.
Pears	Vitamins – riboflavin (B2), pantothenic acid, folate, C, E Minerals – copper, potassium	Help lower cholesterol levels, high in fibre (good for digestion and can help with diarrhoea), help prevent high blood pressure.
Oranges (with seeds and peel removed)	Vitamins – A, thiamin (B1), C Minerals – calcium, copper, potassium	Help maintain cholesterol levels. Good source of Vitamin C, which boosts the immune system.

Food	Vitamins and minerals	Benefits
Honey	Vitamins – pantothenic acid, B6 Minerals – calcium, copper, iron, magnesium, manganese, phosphorus, potassium, sodium, zinc	Boosts energy, and local honey may help tackle allergies. Good for skin condition and the immune system.
Peanut butter	Vitamins – folate, E Minerals – magnesium, copper, phosphorus, manganese	Good source of protein, good for skin health. Provides slow-release energy. Contains fibre (good for digestion and can help with diarrhoea).
Brown rice	Vitamins – thiamin (B1), niacin (B3), B6 Minerals – magnesium, phosphorus, selenium, manganese	Selenium helps reduce cancer risk. Good for mopping up toxins and normalising cholesterol levels.
Carrots	Vitamins – A, thiamin (B1), riboflavin (B2), niacin (B3), B6, C, E and K Minerals – potassium, cobalt, iron, magnesium, copper, iodine, phosphorus	Benefit eye health, good source of antioxidants. Good for bone strength and kidney health, blood clotting factors and maintaining a healthy immune system.

Common problems you can kiss goodbye to with a change of diet

I promise you that by changing your dog's diet, not giving up at the first hurdle and having a little faith in yourself, you can substantially, if not entirely, rid your dog of the following:

- Wind
- Bad breath
- Overgrowth of *Candida* (yeast)
- Loose stools
- Poor coat condition
- That doggy smell
- Constipation

If you have a dog with any, or all, of these culprits try the following:

- Change your dog food to one with better ingredients and less carbohydrate (more on this below). I'd ditch kibble in favour of a combination of a good wet food and home cooking, and/or add raw feeding too.
- Add a mixture of probiotics and prebiotics to her diet for a few weeks to help restore the gut flora to health – try Lintbells' YuDIGEST or Bionic Biotic from Pooch & Mutt.
- Add Dorwest Tree Barks Powder to food daily – try a mix of slippery elm and white poplar bark. This re-

duces inflammation in the gut, allows better absorption of nutrients and firms up loose stools.

- Replace your dog treats with Feelwell's probiotic dog treats – one month on a bag of these bad boys her wind will be much improved.

- For the long term I would put a dog on Dorwest Keeper's Mix, which is a blend of kelp, celery seeds, alfalfa, nettles, rosemary, psyllium husks, cleavers and wild yam. Each herb works on a different part of the dog – rosemary for digestion and wind, psyllium for bowel health and digestion and wild yam to maintain healthy intestines. Keeper's Mix is a very all-round good supplement and can be taken alongside any medication.

- If constipation is your dog's problem, get more veg into her. Dorwest's Mixed Vegetable tablets are good too, but as a supplement, not a replacement for veg.

A note on probiotics

Please don't give your dog a probiotic made for humans. A customer called recently to say she was giving her dog a well-known drink that contains lots of "good bacteria". She wanted to know if it would help her dog's digestive 'issues'. I had to say that it probably wouldn't – mainly because it contains not one, but three types of sugar. A dog's gut doesn't like sugar; it's one of the main causes of an upset stomach, which then leads to the problems that the 'good bacteria' are meant to sort out. Even for humans, the average probiotic drink is probably one of the most counterintuitive food products I've ever come across. Don't waste your money.

Whichever dog-specific probiotic you're thinking of giving yours, take a really good look at the label. The first ingredients listed must be prebiotic and probiotic. I just looked at the ingredients of one probiotic made for dogs and first on the list were meat and animal derivatives. If you're trying to improve your dog's gut health, this isn't what you need to see.

The carbohydrate conundrum

Carbohydrates provide energy. I'll stick my neck out and say I bet that a few of you reading this will have tried losing weight on a zero-carb diet at some point. If you managed to stick to the diet, I expect you lost a shed-load of weight – I certainly did. How long did it take you to put it all back on, and then some? For me it was about a year. While following this type of diet slavishly will make the weight drop off, it's not sustainable, and there is research to show we can damage our heart and kidneys eating mostly protein over the long term. HOWEVER, you should ditch cheap, processed, refined carbohydrates from your diet. They play havoc with our pancreas, liver, digestion and endocrine systems and lead to lethargy, obesity, type 2 diabetes, heart disease and arthritis. And it's exactly the same for our dogs and cats.

Refined carbohydrates are found in anything processed and on the beige end of the colour spectrum (white flours, sugar, crisps, sweets, biscuits, cakes) and in large quantities in dry dog food! They break down into simple sugars very easily in a dog's digestive system and lead to an overgrowth of *Candida* yeast, which thrives on sugars.

On the other hand, complex carbohydrates are king. Their nutritional benefits are legion; they provide slow-release energy, aid digestion, help regulate metabolism, improve sleep function, keep the immune system strong and the nervous system in shape. Complex carbohydrates come from unprocessed or whole foods such as fresh vegetables, fruit, brown rice, quinoa, whole oats, pearl barley and sweet potato.

Carbs and weight control for dogs

If you feed your dog good (complex) carbohydrates, in smaller quantities, the weight will come off slowly and stay off. There is plenty of research to show that a low-carbohydrate, high-fat, fruit-and-vegetable diet results in sustained weight loss. So I say this with conviction:

ditch the dry food, or kibble, as much as possible (and it's entirely possible) – even if it's top-notch kibble. It doesn't matter how good the carbohydrate source was when it started out, by the time it's gone through the cooking process it will have become a refined carbohydrate. Put simply, it's a dog food version of our biscuits, breakfast cereal or pasta that becomes a 'complete food' once all the vitamins and minerals have been added.

When I ask customers what they're feeding their dog, they often say 'hardly anything and she's still putting on weight, and begging for food!' This doesn't surprise me if a dog is eating only kibble. The refined carbohydrates play havoc with a dog's blood sugar (and insulin) levels, which shoot up fast after eating, then plummet just as speedily a short while later so you end up with a dog in a sugar trough, begging for more food.

Uncooked carbohydrate

The ingredient that really irritates your dog's gut is raw starch. This is because the bad bacteria in your dog's gut thrive on raw starch and can overwhelm the good bacteria, leading to all sorts of problems from bad breath and wind to colitis and skin conditions. You might think that you're not feeding raw starch to your dog, but actually there's uncooked carbohydrate in kibble. And there's more of it in dog food these days because new recipes with higher protein and fat content are being cooked in machinery not built to handle these changes.

Most kibble is made by extrusion, a process unchanged in decades. The ingredients are mixed together and ground, then cooked under steam and pushed through an extruder. The extruder works using friction, which builds heat, to cook the mixture resulting in a digestible, gelatinised end product. The higher protein and fat content in the new foods means the extruder can't cook the carbs properly so they won't be 100 per cent gelatinised. Most producers aim for 95 per cent of the carbohydrates to be cooked, but if it's below say, 80 per cent, you will end up with at least 20 per cent raw starch content, which can have a significant impact on your dog. It won't matter how much probiotic you add to her dinner if she's getting that amount of raw starch in her bowl.

Testing kibble for uncooked carbs

Take a small handful of kibble, cover it in hot water and leave it for 20 minutes – the kibble should absorb all the water. Now squeeze it to wring out the water. If it contains all cooked starch, there should be no hard bits the kibble should remain intact, and not turn to porridge.

Hard bits left behind are uncooked starch and you should look at changing the food if it's causing a problem in your dog.

Another way to check kibble is to snap a piece in half. You should be able to see all the little holes where the starches have cooked properly. Uncooked starch is denser and biscuit-like.

Obesity and weight control

Keeping the weight off your dog is key to having a healthier, livelier pet, for longer. The less weight his frame is carrying, the easier it is for him to get up and down the stairs (and hills) and the less pressure is added to every step. This means less pain and less wear and tear, slowing degeneration as much as possible.

Did you know that too much fat in the body leads to inflammation of the joint tissues? I blame Green & Black's, Ben & Jerry's and Pieminister (not necessarily in that order) for my fat backside, but of course the fault lies entirely with me. If I feed my dog the wrong food and she gets fat it's also down to me, not her. But what does a dog's proper weight look like? Have a look at the chart overleaf. I know some of you will be surprised.

Don't let the ribs scare you

A few years ago, someone reported my sister to the RSPCA, concerned that her Lurcher, Bud, was being starved. The inspector took one look at Bud, turned around and left, casting a casual 'He looks like a Lurcher is supposed to' glance over his shoulder. What he meant is, you could clearly see his ribs. Bud wasn't a bag of bones and you couldn't see his hips from space the way you can on a poor starved creature. He looked just right.

On the other hand, I met a lady with Greyhounds at a dog show who said she liked her dogs to have some fat on them. She didn't like seeing any bones, because her perception was that visible bones in this day and age denote neglect, and she thought it was healthier if her dog was fat. With dogs, just as with humans, we've lost perspective on what a healthy weight looks like. However, it's far easier to keep an eye on your dog's weight than on your own – or at least it is in my case.

Don't be afraid of change

If your dog is overweight, don't be scared to have a really good look at his diet and change it if you need to. If he's been eating the same thing year after year he may well get a mild case of diarrhoea for a couple of days as his gut is getting used to the change, but this soon passes.

I'm going to stick my neck out and say that you don't have to listen to your vet, the pet shop, or anyone else who says that your dog must eat the same food every day, without deviation – or that he must be given an expensive prescription-only food. Once you've read through this section, contact me if you have any questions or need advice on how to go about changing your dog's diet.

WHAT SHAPE IS YOUR DOG?

A little extra weight can be a **BIG PROBLEM**.

Whether it's once a week or once a month, check your dog's body score regularly to make sure he's staying happy and healthy.

BODY 1 SCORE
VERY THIN
<5% body fat

Ribs
Easily felt with no fat cover

Tail Base
Bones are raised, no fat cover

Side View
Severe abdominal tuck

Overhead View
Accentuated hourglass shape

20% below ideal body weight

Consult your veterinarian!

BODY 2 SCORE
UNDERWEIGHT
5-15% body fat

Ribs
Easily felt with little fat cover

Tail Base
Bones are raised with slight fat cover

Side View
Abdominal tuck

Overhead View
Marked hourglass shape

10% below ideal body weight

Consult your veterinarian to see if you are underfeeding your dog

---

BODY 3 SCORE
IDEAL BODY WEIGHT
16-25% body fat

Ribs
Easily felt with slight fat cover

Tail Base
Some contour with slight fat cover

Side View
Abdominal tuck

Overhead View
Well-proportioned waist

Ideal body weight

Great job!
Keep doing what you are doing

BODY 4 SCORE
OVERWEIGHT
26-35% body fat

Ribs
Difficult to feel under moderate fat cover

Tail Base
Some thickening, bones palpable under moderate fat cover

Side View
No abdominal tuck

Overhead View
Back is slightly broadened at waist

10% above ideal body weight

Consult your veterinarian about the right nutrition for your dog and about ways to increase activity

---

BODY 5 SCORE
OBESE
> 35% body fat

Ribs
Difficult to feel under thick fat cover

Tail Base
Thickened and difficult to feel under thick fat cover

Side View
No waist, fat hangs from abdomen

Overhead View
Back is markedly broadened

20% above ideal body weight

Extra weight can cause serious health problems for your dog. Consult your veterinarian about the right nutrition for your dog

It winds me up that the diet industry with its 'eat this or you're doing it wrong' mentality has seeped into the pet food industry. It's made us fearful of following our gut instincts and eroded our confidence. Change your dog's diet, choose better foods, cut out calories she doesn't need and most importantly, exercise her more. If you need help, just ask. Many vets run weight clinics, so use them for their advice and support – but go your own way on food. Your dog will be happier for it and I guarantee you'll save money too.

CHAPTER 5

ALLERGIES

After queries about itchy skin, the most common conversation I have with first-time customers, by miles, is about allergies. Many worried owners call to enquire about dog treats. They've had allergy testing done on their dog, either blood sampling or full-on skin testing under sedation (see page 90), and it turns out 'that my dog is allergic to everything – pork, beef, chicken; wheat, barley and maize; house, dust and storage mites; grasses and pollens. You name it, my dog's allergic to it. So what dog treats can he eat?' 'Err... sweet potato?' comes my weedy answer.

Is it actually an allergy?

I've always thought, it can't be right that all these dogs are truly allergic to all these things. There must be degrees of reactivity a dog may not have developed a full allergy, but has reacted negatively to certain things. Some reactions must simply be an intolerance, or a sensitivity, to something. And it turns out I'm right. I asked professional allergy testers and here's what they told me: 'If your dog is having a reaction to something, however mild, understandably you want to know what triggers it. Symptoms might be vomiting, itching and scratching, runny eyes and nose or smelly, itchy ears. The most common symptoms are classified into three groups: dermatological (the skin), gastrointestinal (the gut) and respiratory (the lungs, nose and throat). Symptoms begin when the body starts to think that something normal and everyday – a food or pollen, for example – is now dangerous. The reaction – the itching or vomiting – is the body's way of speaking up. It's the smoke signal sent up to let you know that there's trouble in paradise.'

It is estimated that 10-15 per cent of the canine population in the UK suffer from atopy (a reaction to certain substances) at one time or another. Many atopic reactions start in hood and the dog grows out of it as she reaches adulthood, just as we do.

What is an allergy?

A true allergy occurs when the immune system reacts abnormally to common, usually harmless, substances, for example, pollen, food or insects. It can be genetic (inherited), which means it will affect your dog for all his life and will need managing. However, if your dog merely suffers an adverse reaction to something - a food, say - or builds up an intolerance, the resulting problem will generally be confined to the digestive system; whereas a full-blown allergic reaction will trigger a strong immune response that could be life threatening.

How do you know if your dog has a food intolerance rather than an allergy?

Well, every dog has his own 'critical threshold' – the point at which exposure to several allergens causes the level of stimulation to build up, pushing him over the edge, resulting in a flare-up. To make matters more confusing, these thresholds vary from dog to dog. It can depend on his breeding, environment, vaccine history, diet – you name it, it can have an effect on tolerance. It is possible to test for allergies, but this should only be done after you've eliminated other possible causes for example a parasitic infection (fleas, mange, etc, see Chapter 2) and you've tried to determine if a certain food is the culprit (see elimination diet, below). What you don't want to do is immediately assume that your dog has an allergy, and so end up making unnecessary and potentially stressful lifelong changes for your dog.

Testing for a food intolerance

There is growing evidence that dogs fed on the same food continuously can develop an adverse food reaction (or ADR) to certain foods. Your dog can be quite happily scoffing bowls of 'I Can't Believe This Is Actual Dog Food' for years and then suddenly start to itch, scratch, smell, and, for good measure, get the runs. If you think your dog might have developed a food intolerance, congratulations, you are today's winner as weeding out a dietary problem is going to be way easier than keeping a dog away from grass and tree pollen.

If you suspect food is the problem, the way to sort it out is with an elimination diet. You do have to be strong in the face of those big brown eyes and steel yourself against any begging or emotional connection you have to food. Try not to project your feelings onto your dog, like the rest of us do – this is the time for fortitude and tough love.

The elimination diet

An elimination diet works like this. For 8 to 12 weeks feed your dog a protein and a carbohydrate source she doesn't normally eat or hasn't eaten before; for instance, if your dog eats chicken and rice, then try him on fish and sweet potato and absolutely nothing else. With a bit of luck, you'll be able to select the foods that are least likely to cause a problem. Stick to this diet (plus water) – no treats, no titbits, no sneaking him a bit of food under the table at mealtimes – simple, and yet really hard all at once. It's simple because you know where you are and what you're feeding your dog. It's hard because you have to get everyone in the house on board, keep all other food away from a pleading dog, and be able to resist that wistful stare. The simple fact of the matter is, if you adhere to with the elimination diet it's impossible to tell whether your dog has a food intolerance or allergy at all, or if it's the 'snacks' that are causing the symptoms. Be strong, be the grown-up, and reward yourself with a large glass of something on the first day that you're not confronted with a large pile of sloppy, stinky, blood-infused poo. Rejoice in a firm stool, people!

If this approach clears up the symptoms, it's pretty safe to say that it's food that is causing your dog's issues. At the very least it's certainly not contributing to tipping him over the edge into a crisis, which is good news all round.

Once you've established that your dog's symptoms go away when he's fed only two foods and water, the next step is to start introducing new foods, one at a time. If you've been giving him chicken and rice, try adding lamb, and see what happens. If there's no change, introduce fish and rice, then try fish and green beans. It's key that you make one change at a time, otherwise, if the symptoms reappear, you won't know which food is stirring up trouble. If you get a reaction to a food, make a note of it and don't feed it to your dog ever again. Over time, you'll end up with a list of foods that don't trigger a reaction and can be safely fed to your dog.

The golden rule

If you have established that your dog has a food intolerance and you want to go back to feeding shop-bought dog food, always read the labels and choose one that lists individual ingredients by name, for example chicken, lamb, salmon. That way you can make sure you're not feeding your dog a problem ingredient. Never, ever, go back to one that lists them by category, for example, 'meat and animal derivatives', as you won't know if it includes the problem ingredient(s) that could make the symptoms reappear. And don't forget, the same goes for treats.

Allergy testing

If an elimination diet has not helped, it could well be time for an allergy test. There are two types: serological allergy testing – i.e. a blood test; and intradermal testing – a skin test. Blood tests are carried out first, as skin testing requires your dog to be sedated. In both tests, your vet is looking for potential allergens and the antibodies they produce that could be responsible for the adverse reaction in your dog.

Almost anything can be an allergen but the most common are house dust mites, pollens and food, animal dander and insects. In the presence of an allergen, the immune system produces antibodies known as immuno-globulins; allergy tests look for the proteins that make up these immunoglobulins. For example, in the case of digestive problems, an allergy test might look for an intolerance to lactose (milk sugars), food additives or histamine-releasing foods.

Here comes the science

Blood serum taken from your dog is diluted and intro-duced to a panel of allergens on a micro-titre plate (looks a bit like a Connect 4 game, only smaller and horizontal). There are three specific panels to choose from:

- Foods – meats, cereals, eggs, milk
- Environmental – grass, trees, weeds, pollens
- Secondary infection – *Malassezia* and sarcoptic mange

The test reproduces what happens when an adverse reaction occurs in your dog, and then measures the antigens (an allergen that produces an abnormally strong response) and antibodies produced in the sample. The allergic response is graded according to the numbers of antigens and antibodies produced, on a scale of one.

Understanding the results

So you have your allergy testing back from the vet and you've got a reaction of two for chicken, three for potato and five for beef. Then a four for meadow grass and a three for nettle. But it doesn't necessarily mean that your dog is allergic to all these things. Your dog may have scored a two on chicken and that low number will be enough to have him pulling his fur out, but his score of four on meadow grass triggers absolutely no reaction whatsoever. All it means is that antibodies have been detected by the test – your dog has had an immune response to something her system used to see as normal, but now views as the enemy.

To make matters even more confusing, these results can be skewed by many factors including recent vaccinations or a change in his environment. Perhaps you have moved from the coast to the countryside, or a new person or pet has moved into the house.

All I can tell you is that allergy testing is your starting point. It doesn't provide all the answers. Your dog may also have more than one allergy, and it could be that it's the combination that's pushing him over the threshold.

Immunotherapy injections

If, through allergy testing, luck and a following wind, you and your vet have managed to pin down one or more specific non-food allergens that are triggering your dog's reactions (pollen, timothy grass or house dust mites, for instance), then a course of immunotherapy injections could reduce symptoms. It's unlikely that immuno-therapy will cure your dog's allergy, but it can get it to a stage where she only has the odd, manageable flare-up.

Put simply, immunotherapy treats the disease with substances that stimulate the immune response. For example, my mate Jerry is allergic to pet hair and yet he has a cat. I can pick up his cat, bury my face in her fur, inhale her lovely kitty smell and I come away with only a rude stare. If Jerry did this his immune system would be in a flat spin, with a very severe allergic reaction – he'd be on oxygen in the back of an ambulance on his way to A&E. So why does he have a cat, you may ask? Jerry knew he was allergic to cats, but decided to get one anyway, figuring that with constant exposure to the dander and fur, his lungs would become used to it. After a while his immune response calmed down and they live happily together. But it only works with his own cat – and at arm's length! At my house you can always tell where Jerry is, just by following the sounds of coughing and snottiness as my cat Pearl's fur finds its way up his nose. However, Jerry's still alive and his cat Dusty has reached the ripe old age of 20 – too old to run away from me and my fur-inhaling ways, much as she would like to.

In a similar way, immunotherapy injections introduce tiny amounts of an allergen to your dog's immune system. If, for example, your dog reacts to timothy grass, over the course of the injections his itching and scratching will lessen and flare-ups will be moderate and occasional rather than severe. The vet will get the vial made up to your dog's specific requirements and keep it in the fridge ready for when you bring him in. Alternatively, you could try doing it yourself at home. Your vet will show you how it's done. It can be a lot cheaper for you and less stressful for the dog.

Products that can make life easier for your dog

Some of these products help reduce the symptoms of a chronic, ongoing problem, and others can be used when your dog has a flare-up.

The products I've listed for external use will calm down itching skin, eyes and ears so your poor dog isn't scratching herself to bits. If she does end up drawing blood, the neem oil will help her to heal quickly.

Then there are food supplements. Add fish and coconut oils every day as a matter of course, and Dorwest's Tree Barks probiotics when your dog has a gastrointestinal flare-up – you know the score, stomach cramps and whimpering followed by a full-on yucky deluge. A day or so on this, along with a bland diet, will right most sinking ships!

Products for external use	What's it good for?	When to use
CSJ's Skinny Spray – contains neem seed extract	Soothes itching and/or sore skin and it's a great insect repellent.	Use daily until itching subsides
Colloidal silver eye spray	Relieves itching eyes. Use to clean minor eye irritations from pollen and dust. Clears away tear stains.	As necessary
Colloidal silver ear drops	Use for crud and bacteria-busting ear cleaning caused by allergies, yeast problems or mites.	As necessary
Neem oil / Ekoneem	Brilliant for treating yeasty skin, bites, wounds, scratches and minor infections and as an insect repellent.	As necessary

Supplements	What's it good for?	When to use
Omega oils 3 and 6 – YuMEGA Itchy Dog	Eases dry skin, reduces moult and symptoms of allergies.	Add daily to food

Virgin coconut oil – Cocomutts is good	Strengthens immune system, improves digestion, and great for skin health.	Add daily to food
Probiotic YuDIGEST or Bionic Biotic	Restores good gut health especially after illness and medication and improves *Candida* (yeast) overgrowth on skin and in ears.	Give daily until no longer needed
Dorwest Tree Barks Powder	Relieves an inflamed gut, helps your dog absorb nutrients and reduces the runs!	Give daily until no longer needed

CHAPTER 6

EARS AND EYES

Dog's ears come in all shapes and sizes, from the short and open to the oh-so-long (think Basset Hound), from the practically hairless inside to the impenetrable forest of fur, and everything in between. Some breeds are more prone to ear problems than others.

In this section I will also talk briefly about common eye problems and the natural ways to maintain good eye health, including some easy first-aid fixes. Anything else should be seen by a vet.

All about ears

You can tell a lot about a dog's mood by watching her ears. If she is on to something, a hint of a squirrel maybe, her ears will be erect and facing forward. If her ears are pulled back a bit she is pleased to see you and relaxed. If she has had enough or something is upsetting her mojo, her ears will be laid back against her head, meaning, 'I don't like this'. And very often you'll see dogs moving their ears independently of each another.

Dogs have incredibly good hearing; they can detect sounds at such a high frequency that they can hear an insect walking. Dogs know when we're in mortal danger even when we are oblivious to it – for mortal danger read small child walking past your window, of course!

Dogs with long ears, narrow ear canals and those with allergies are more prone to ear problems, but most will have an issue at some point or another. Bacteria and overgrowth of *Candida* yeast are the primary causes of ear infections in dogs. Chuck in your ear mites, cysts, tumours, trapped water and/or grass seeds, a build-up of ear wax and too much ear hair and it's no wonder ears are the number one reason why your dog ends up at the vet. The following signs indicate that your dog has an ear problem:

- More ear scratching than usual
- Smelly ears
- Head shaking
- Redness or wounds inside the ear flap
- Rubbing ears along the floor or walls
- Hair loss around the ear
- Hearing loss
- Discharge

Given that your dog is likely to have to submit to having

his ears poked around at some point, it's a good idea to get him used to having his ears touched and examined when there isn't a problem. That way your dog is less inclined to object and/or bite you when something is sore and you need to have a look inside.

How to clean your dog's ears

If you like cleaning your dog's ears, and your dog likes having them cleaned, the satisfaction to effort ratio is out of this world. Especially if your dog is a dirt magnet. The best tip I had from my vet was that you should only clean where you can actually see – don't ever push anything down into the ear canal. She had a 'don't mess with me' look in her eye when she said it, which I respect enormously. It's good advice, so don't.

When you look down into the ear canal you'll see it appears to stop at a dead end. In actual fact, the ear canal just turns at a right angle in towards your dog's head. Never try to go around the bend with any foreign object.

You can do a simple wash with salty water or apple cider vinegar diluted with warm water. Or, for itchy, mucky ears, colloidal silver ear drops work very well. Squeeze a few drops from a dropper bottle into your dog's ear and quickly start to massage the base of the ear from the outside. Keep a firm hold on the dog while you do this, otherwise you'll end up picking bits of ear crud off your nice clean shirt as your dog shakes her head. Next, clean out the ear with an ear-cleaning cloth, a ball of cotton wool or soft kitchen paper (again, only as far as you can see, and no poking about with a cotton bud). Clean off as much crud as you can. Then let the dog go and stand well back. If your dog shakes her head vigorously it will bring more waxy dirt up from the depths, which you can then clear out with more cotton wool. I find it revolting, but oddly satisfying. This whole matter is probably best dealt with outside, come to think of it.

If your dog is of the hair-growing, non-moulting variety, you're probably a regular at the groomers, anyway – ask them to pay special attention to ear cleaning. Clean your dog's ears at home on a regular basis, too. If you do a little light clipping of ear hair at the same time it helps to maintain airflow inside the ear. Ask your groomer to show you a safe way to do it.

Ear infections

Ear infections come in two flavours: acute (sudden onset) and chronic (long term). Treatment is the same for both types of infection, but if your dog has a recurring problem, that will need looking at too. It may be that a change of diet is in order, or simply that you're not getting your Cocker Spaniel's ears really dry after a swim, for example.

Tips for preventing ear infections

- Check ears regularly for smells, mites, dirt or wax build-up
- Clean them if they appear dirty
- Dry ears thoroughly but gently after a bath or swim
- Remove excess ear hair or ask the groomer to do it for you

Acute ear infection

An acute ear infection can be the result of a bite or cut, or it can follow an ear mite infestation, which can result in a bacterial infection and need to be treated with a short course of antibiotics. Signs of acute infection include redness on the skin either inside or outside the ear, and if it's mites, you'll see a brown, greasy film inside the ears and there may a musty smell, too.

Chronic ear infection

A chronic ear infection is one that just won't quit, no matter what you throw at it or for how long. This is more common among dogs with allergies and those suffering with weakened immune systems, often caused by stress, a poor diet or overuse of antibiotics. Often the ears are red, sore and smelly, especially if the infection is caused by a chronic overgrowth of yeast (*Candida*) resulting from a diet high in processed carbohydrate (see page 15 for more on this subject).

Tips for cleaning up ear problems

- Use neem oil on reddened, sore areas and open wounds.
- A few drops of colloidal silver into the ear followed by a good clean will clear up bacteria and minor infections very well.
- Use cider vinegar diluted with warm water as a soothing wash inside ears and ear flaps. This is lovely mixed with cool water (not freezing cold) for relief on a hot day too.
- If your dog has a weakened immune system caused by stress, a period of illness or long-term use of medication, a short course of an echinacea supplement will help strengthen his body and enable him to fend off infections. Try CSJ's Resist!
- If the ear infection results from a recurring yeast problem, then it's time to look at reducing stress, changing diet and strengthening your dog's immune system. Addressing the former two should go a long way towards resolving the latter.

Ear mites

Ear mites present as a reddish-brown waxy substance that can easily be mistaken for dirt. Wipe a bit out with your finger if you can stomach it (I love it, but I'm weird) and rub it between your fingers. If it's greasy it's probably ear mites.

What you can do to help

Either clean the ears out with colloidal silver drops and an ear-cleaning cloth (see above) or dust the inside of the inner ear with Thornit powder – both have good anti-bacterial properties. My personal choice is silver drops because I can drop them down into the ear and let them work their way into places I can't (and wouldn't want to) poke about in, and it's less messy. Either will work just fine, though.

My cat Dave used to suffer from ear mites. I have no idea why as he never attracted fleas, ticks or other parasites. Luckily for me, he loved having his ears cleaned – I think it just made them feel so much better afterwards. There's nothing like sticking a wodge of kitchen towel doused in colloidal silver into your cat's ear, for him to ram his head as hard as he can into your finger for maximum satisfaction. Like I said, I'm weird.

Fungus in the ears

If you smell a yeasty odour when you put your nose to your dog's ear, he probably has a fungal problem caused by an overgrowth of the yeast *Candida albicans* (candidiasis). When *Candida* proliferates in the gut unchecked it can lead to an overgrowth that turns up in the ears.

What you can do to help

Add a probiotic, short-term, to your dog's diet and eliminate sugars and over-processed carbohydrates for a while. It's back to reading those dog food labels for you. Clean the ears daily for a few days with colloidal silver drops and an ear-cleaning cloth or apply a thin film of neem oil to any red or spotty patches.

Blockages in the ears

Blockages can be caused by excess hair and wax build-up, grass seeds or water. Just like old men, dogs, especially those that don't moult – Bedlington Terriers, Poodles, Bichon Frises, for example – collect ear hair like some people collect stamps. When it gets tangled up with excess earwax you're on your way to a great ear-cleaning session!

What you can do to help

If you think there is a foreign body, such as a grass seed, in your dog's ear, then, unless it's so loose and near the top of the ear you can pick it off easily, take your dog to the vet or groomer to get it removed.

Eye problems

Eyes are not to be trifled with and I always get any eye problems other than general maintenance and cleaning checked out at the vet. The problem could be a scratched cornea, cyst, conjunctivitis (inflammation of the outer covering of the eye – conjunctiva), an infection of the third eyelid, glaucoma (a condition of increased pressure within the eyeball, which causes gradual loss of sight), cataracts (where the lens gradually becomes opaque), retinal detachment – you get the idea. These are not conditions you're going to be able to diagnose, let alone treat, on your own. Some breeds are more prone to certain diseases than others. For example Basset Hounds, Great Danes and Cocker Spaniels are susceptible to glaucoma. West Highland Whites, Yorkshire terriers and Cavalier King Charles Spaniels are susceptible to conjunctivitis.

Eye problems can occur in utero, in puppies, as a result of injury or infection, poor nutrition or old age, so it's always good to get any changes to your dog's eyes checked out immediately. Problems that develop inside the eye or under the eyelid can fall under the radar. What looks like a minor irritation could be causing a lot of damage, and you don't want that going undetected. Dogs may have dry or watery eyes, rub their eyes with their forelegs, scratch them with their claws – thus adding bacteria to the mix – or shy away from bright light.

Watery eyes

Nikita often gets itchy, watery eyes, especially if we've been out on the Downs for the afternoon. It's probably all the pollen and dust swirling about – she's barely 60cm (2ft) off the ground after all. If I leave them she'll start licking her forelegs, then using them to rub her eyes. Lord knows what bacteria lurk in that mouth.

What you can do to help
I use a colloidal silver spray (try Lintbells' Silvercare) to wipe her eyes clean and over-the-counter eye drops with added antihistamine from an optician. The vet recommended the latter to me and it really helps.

Dry eyes

Our dog BB was born with only one tear duct so one of her eyes is constantly dry and collects debris that she can't get rid of through normal tear action.

What you can do to help
We clean BB's ears using false tears, recommended by the vet, but again purchased from the optician. It seems to work and doesn't bother her at all.

Tear staining

There are small holes called puncta near each eye that drain tears away and down the throat. If the eye gets too irritated – from an ingrown hair or a turned-in eyelid, for instance – these can get blocked, leading to more tears spilling out, which in turn leads to staining. It is much more noticeable in fair-furred breeds such as West Highland Whites.

What you can do to help
Again, colloidal silver used daily to remove tears from fur will reduce the staining until it's gone completely.

Monitor eye health

There's not a lot more I can say about eyecare really, in a DIY sense at least, because so much can be happening around and inside the eye that we can't see or diagnose. The only thing to add to the above is that once again, good nutrition plays a key part in keeping your dog's eyes in good health. If it's more than daily care you're worried about, then please do take your dog to your vet.

CHAPTER 7

BONES AND JOINTS

Think how much ground your dog covers compared to you on a walk. You will be walking from A to B and back (around a forest track/along the towpath to the pub and home); your dog, on the other hand, probably runs from A to Z via J to F and back to Z darting backwards and forwards, lowering her head to sniff the ground. Your dog may run at full pelt from a standing start, swerve at extremely short notice to avoid obstacles, or just smack straight into whatever's in the way, usually you. She will chase balls, people, seagulls – basically anything that moves. As a result, her joints really take a pounding every day.

Mobility is incredibly important to dogs and you need to look for subtle signs that indicate there's a problem because, as we know, dogs hide pain to avoid appearing weak. If it looks like your dog is finding it hard work to get out of bed, lie down, go upstairs or get into the car – or she's developed a rolling gait – then it's time for a check-up. Many mobility problems – whether or not they have to be treated surgically – will need managing for life, through weight maintenance, the right amount of exercise, a good joint supplement and sometimes physical therapy.

Mobility problems in dogs tend to be degenerative, developmental or inherited. And then there are those self-imposed ones, caused, I like to think, by a dog's skewed sense of danger. If I turn around after washing my hands to grab a towel and a drop of water hits Nikita's skin, she thinks the world's just caved in. But if we're on a walk and there's the merest whiff of a fox, she completely loses what scant road sense she has to run across the road without hesitation. Injury can mean all sorts of lasting damage to the joints, tendons and ligaments.

What can go wrong

The most common causes of impaired mobility are:

- Hip dysplasia
- Elbow dysplasia
- Osteoarthritis
- Cruciate ligament injury leading to secondary arthritis
- Hind limb lameness
- Knee and ankle problems
- Shoulder problems – as dogs have no collar bones

these are mostly ligament and tendon problems
• Disc herniation

Your dog may have joint pain if you see any of the following signs:

• Lameness – your dog holds a limb up, avoids bearing weight on one leg
• Does not run as far or as fast as she used to
• Difficulty jumping up on things that were previously not a problem
• Lack of interest in the activities she used to love
• Licking a particular spot, an elbow, for instance

I'm not going to discuss possible surgery, anti-inflammatory medication or any other type of veterinary treatment your dog may need in this book. That's between you and your vet. I'm going to tell you about prevention strategies and ways of managing lameness or long-term joint problems at home.

Hip dysplasia

This is the most common mobility complaint in dogs. It is inherited. Although not present at birth, it evolves over the first few months, coming to light at between 6 and 12 months of age. It happens when the ball-and-socket joint at the hip grows in a deformed way – the socket resembles a saucer while the 'ball' part at the top of the bone grows with a flat top. It's most common in large or fast-growing dogs. If your dog has hip dysplasia, he is almost certainly going to develop arthritis too – joy of joys. It's likely to affect both hips and treatment depends on the severity of the pain and how badly mobility is affected.

What you can do to help

This is definitely one for the vet, but a top-notch mobility supplement can really help alleviate some of the symptoms. Add Lintbells' YuMOVE joint supplement to your dog's food or give it as a treat every day; it's the bestselling joint supplement in the UK because it really works. Keeping your dog's weight down will also improve his symptoms.

Elbow dysplasia

This is another genetic condition in which the three bones that make up the elbow don't fit together properly, putting undue pressure onto certain areas. This causes inflammation, osteoarthritis and degenerative injuries such as stress fractures and cartilage erosion. Surgery isn't common, though arthroscopy (a peek inside the elbow using a tiny camera) is performed on dogs more commonly now.

What you can do to help
As with hip dysphasia, weight management and good supplements like Lintbells' YuMOVE for joint health and Dorwest Mixed Vegetable tablets will help to reduce the pain and inflammation significantly.

Cruciate ligament injury

This is a long-term degenerative injury in dogs. Our cruciate ligaments snap following a high-impact injury, often sports-related, whereas a dog's wear over time. The cruciate ligament is a band of fibrous tissue that attaches the thigh bone to the shin bone over the knee (there's a song in there somewhere), and in dogs it wears away, like a fraying rope.

What you can do to help
This is one for the vet as it's an injury that responds very well to surgery.

Osteoarthritis

This degrades the fluid cushion that protects joints, synovial fluid, tendons, ligaments and cartilage.

What you can do to help
A daily dose of Lintbells' YuMOVE or CSJ's No Ake will work to slow the degradation process and offer relief for the symptoms of osteoarthritis. Weight management helps here too.

Degenerative problems

Have you ever seen an old man and his old dog keeping each other company as they take themselves for a twirl around the park? Chances are they're both suffering from age-related degeneration of the hips, knees and spine. Crumbly old bones are just a fact of life, but those turns around the park are going a long way towards keeping them helahty and mobile.

What you can do to help
As well as keeping your dog moving at a gentle pace and watching his weight, you can give him some supplements, such as Lintbells' YuMOVE or CSJ's No Ake

– they really do work – and perhaps some omega 3 and 6 oil. Physical therapies such as hydrotherapy, massage and even acupuncture can be effective too (see below). I have started using light therapy on Nikita (see page opposite) – it's worked wonders for my cat Pearl.

Physical therapies that can help

Go for physiotherapy or other options such as acupuncture only if they're recommended by your vet, and discuss your dog's symptoms with the practitioner. If your dog likes water you could consider some hydrotherapy. Muscles have to work extra hard if they're compensating for aching, degenerating bones, so reducing the weight load in the water is a brilliant way to improve mobility and relieve pain. Hydrotherapy helps rebuild lost muscle and tone when stiff joints mean he's not able to exercise as much. Massage is good too as it releases toxins stored in muscles, leaving your dog relieved and relaxed at the same time.

Acupuncture has a sound, well-documented place in science. It is now widely believed to stimulate the body's repair mechanisms, including the nervous system. And it is gaining popularity among dog owners, especially to help with pain and nerve damage. However, it should be noted that it is illegal in the UK for anyone other than a veterinary surgeon qualified in acupuncture to treat animals. Always ask to see the practitioner's qualifications.

Light therapy

Another thing I'm starting to use on Nikita, which I already use on my cat Pearl, is red-light therapy. It's fairly new to the UK, in dog terms at least, but there is strong scientific evidence for its benefits. It has really helped Pearl's old bones, and you can do it yourself at home. Light therapy works by sending out specific wavelengths of red and infrared light through LEDs. When we get older our cells take longer to repair and the red light helps the cells to heal faster. Red-light therapy reduces inflammation and swelling, thereby reducing pain and stress. It also increases lymphatic activity, allowing toxins to drain more easily from the body.

You can use red-light therapy for arthritis, joint dysplasia, tendonitis, sprains and strains, bruising, inflammation and muscle damage, among other conditions. A word of caution, though: you want to make sure the light you're using on the dog (or cat or horse) is the right strength, so don't buy a cheap device. Go to a reputable supplier and speak to them before buying. If they simply tell you it's an amazing piece of kit, but can't really say why, go elsewhere. I use the Photizo device from www.danetrehealthproducts.com, run by Ruth, the only UK distributor, and it cost me £249. I like Ruth because she really knows her products, and her products work. It's a big upfront cost, but considering how much a vet visit costs and the relief it gives to Pearl, I think it's worth the money. Not only that, but by using red light on Pearl's hips I can stop feeding her anti-inflammatories, which can damage the liver, and cost me £20 a month into the bargain.

Joint supplements

Give your dog a good mobility supplement every day. I recommend YuMOVE by Lintbells. I'll explain why in a minute. It will pay off in spades to do your research before you start off on a supplement, especially if it's for life. A product costing £5 or £50 could contain the same poor levels of the key ingredient, so always READ THE LABEL before you buy. There's no point buying a supplement that your dog is just going to pee on the nearest tree.

The ingredients lists on many joint supplements are at best vague and at worst useless, such as chicken 'flavour', calcium carbonate (which is actually chalk) or 'encapsulated fish oil' (fish oil of indeterminate origin and chalk). I expect active ingredients, not flavours, in a supplement. And in a joint supplement, I want to see glucosamine, chondroitin and manganese. Lintbells' YuMOVE has them all.

- **Glucosamine** occurs naturally in the body in the thick fluid around the joints, but stores deplete with age. The glucosamine used in supplements is derived from sea shells. The most popular form is glucosamine sulphate, but glucosamine hydrochloride, or HCL, is being used more often now as it's a more concentrated form of glucosamine and contains less sodium per dose. Giving a supplement helps to retain that joint fluid for as long as possible, keeping the bones apart for longer, thereby reducing wear and pain.
- **Chondroitin** occurs naturally in the cartilage that covers the ends of bones at joints. The source of chondroitin in joint supplements can be contentious – most of it is marine (actually shark fins) or bovine (from cows). Ethically, I don't have a problem with the bovine form because I eat meat and I figure it's only right we should use as much of the beast as possible, and give a silent thanks to it. Shark is a different matter. These creatures are not farmed and I don't want them caught just for their fins. So if you want to avoid chondroitin from sharks steer clear of supplements that contain 'marine' chondroitin. There is an easier way to get it, in the form of green-lipped mussel extract, which also provides omega 3 fatty acids. Green-lipped mussels are all over the place in New Zealand, and they're farmed extensively. (I lived in

New Zealand in the late 90s and then you could collect them at low tide or pick up a bag fresh from the tank for the equivalent of 15p a kilo – no, it's not a typo – in any supermarket. Delicious and very good for you if you don't count the hot chips and freezing cold beer that come with them!)

- **Manganese** is an essential trace nutrient found in bones and connective tissue.
- **Hyaluronic acid** is the main component of synovial fluid which acts as a lubricant in the synovial joints, reducing friction between cartilage and joints.

Put all these elements together and you have a supplement that lubricates joints, slows wear and tear, helps to repair ligaments, reduces inflammation around cartilage and tendons and keeps fluid between the joints as gooey and viscous as possible for as long as possible. All this allows for increased mobility, reduced pain and a better life.

Notice I haven't mentioned chalk or chicken flavour as a recommended ingredient.

CHAPTER 8

TEETH AND GUMS

Writing this book has changed the way I prioritise my dog Nikita's needs over her wants. Mostly she 'wants' her dinner (and mine and the cat's). What she 'needs' are healthy teeth, which she'll sadly never have as when she was found on the street her teeth were already in an awful state, and that damage is irreversible. Her gums, on the other hand, are in tip-top condition.

You've heard the term 'dog breath' – well, Nikita's breath knows no bounds, and that's down to the state of her teeth. They were so bad when she was found that the vet thought she was much older than she is. After a good clean, her age was amended down to six or seven years, but you could see that most of the enamel on her teeth was badly stained and she would lose more teeth further down the line because she had been neglected. So I really need to keep on top of her oral health.

The problem is that I like putting my fingers in her mouth about as much as she likes having them there – which is not at all. But if I don't do it, as the vet has already told me, she will start to lose her top teeth fairly soon. Nikita has her standards; she doesn't want to look like a pucker-mouthed old lady until she actually is one, and probably not even then.

Look after your dog's teeth and gums

Oral health in dogs is often overlooked, or avoided because of its prominence on the icky scale. As a result, more than 70 per cent of dogs in the UK don't have any oral routine at all and 80 per cent of them have signs of gum disease by the age of three. Have you any idea how much poor dental health is worth to the veterinary industry?

Also, it's not always easy to spot a dog with a dental problem. A dog won't come to you pointing at his mouth. A dog is more likely to spend a lot of time licking a paw or foreleg to help with the pain, or dribbling into his bedding. This happened to Lola, my friend Helen's Border Terrier. Helen asked me what I could recommend as Lola was licking one spot on her leg so much her fur was disappearing. I suggested she start by taking her to the vet. Helen took her the next day, and discovered that she had a broken tooth, not a skin problem at all. Lola had kept her discomfort hidden by licking; she's hard-core, but by no means unusual.

There are cost benefits to regular brushing

If you think that getting a tooth-cleaning routine going will be just another expense you can do without, look at the cost benefit of not keeping on top of dental health.

A toothbrush and dog toothpaste cost approximately £30 per year; over the 12-year life of an average dog that's a total of £360. Compare this with the cost of dental treatment that arises from not brushing teeth. Let's say your dog needs three dental cleans instead (and these need to be done under sedation) – that would set you back around £400 each (nope, not kidding) or £1,200 over the 12 years, which is nearly four times the cost of the brushes and paste. Then there's the risk to your dog of the sedation. Alternatively, you might say a daily dental chew will do the job – at today's prices that will also set you back nearly £1,200. Now you're convinced, turn to page 124 for more on cleaning your dog's teeth.

Seaweed supplements

I haven't mentioned seaweed much before now, but this is the place to start as it's an effective, easy fix for teeth. A seaweed supplement, added daily to food, will break down tartar and plaque. It can take anything up to a couple of months to see a big difference, but it's well worth the wait. As it's a supplement, seaweed works systemically, not locally, on the teeth and gums. Compounds in seaweed kill the bacteria that cause plaque and over time they will also whittle away at tartar, which falls from the teeth and is swallowed, another grim fact you didn't want to know. I recommend CSJ's Seaweed & Parsley or ProDen PlaqueOff.

Seaweed has made a massive difference to Nikita's breath, and has kept her teeth clean and her gums free from painful inflammation. Not only that, but it's the cheapest method by far. A Collie, for instance, would get through about £15 worth a year.

There are two caveats to this. First, if your dog has a lot of tartar it may be best to get her teeth cleaned first by the vet then start afresh. Secondly, seaweed has a high iodine content, so it's not suitable for dogs or cats with hyperthyroidism (over-active thyroid) – this mostly affects older cats, but dogs can suffer from it too.

Chews

Hard chews that contain compounds to fight bacteria aren't my favourite thing, mostly because they list meat and animal derivatives in the ingredients and I'm not happy giving something to a dog if I don't know exactly what's in it. If you find one that lists lovely ingredients and a plaque-fighting addition, please let me know because I'll stock it immediately!

Nothing wrong, though, with getting a good chewing action going for cleaning teeth. There are some good, gluten-free, vegetable-based chews called Whimzees; try their Eurostars, which are the same shape as a Dentastix. The thing I like about them is that they list the ingredients in full, not in categories. I also like Nelson's Plaque Crackers, a hard, cottage-cheese-based (yes, really) dog chew.

Bones are great

The only dogs I've ever come across with sparkling teeth are those fed on a raw diet, and it's the bones that do it. All that chewing action helps and there's none of the 'cack' left on the teeth that comes with eating wet or dry food. Bones are really good for cleaning your dog's teeth, but a broken or fractured tooth will cost you a small fortune at the vet's and not inconsiderable pain to your dog – so avoid bones that are too big for her to handle. I get a tray of marrowbones from the butcher for a couple of pounds. I make sure they are big enough not to be a choking hazard; if they're too big I ask him to saw them in half. The bones generally have a little meat on them and Nikita spends a good hour carving the bits off with her teeth. She loves it.

Always feed bones raw, never cooked, and keep an eye on your dog. It's said that chicken bones are too soft to make a difference, dentally speaking, and there's probably some truth in that, but they're certainly not going to do any harm and they're a good starting point. If you're not confident around raw bones, or don't have any outside space, try a deer antler. They don't splinter, don't smell or get sticky, won't stain your carpet and take months to wear down. Pure Dog (the Stag Bar) or Farm Foods (Antlers) are pure deer antler.

Regular brushing is key

I'm afraid so. Common dental problems in dogs start with plaque, which leads to bad breath and inflammation of the gums (gingivitis). Over time this inflammation works its way down into the bone and tooth loss follows. The minute the dog eats, plaque starts to build up, and if you don't brush the plaque off the teeth, it turns to tartar. Plaque can be brushed away, but tartar has to be scraped off – under sedation.

Brushing won't be well received the first time you try it, or the second, but it's something to persevere with. In the long run it will save your dog a lot of pain, by way of infection, sore gums and lost teeth. Furthermore, studies have shown that tooth decay and gum disease can lead to far more serious problems with major organs – heart, liver and kidneys – as bacteria from the gums leak out into the body systems.

How to clean a dog's teeth
Get yourself either a tooth-cleaning cloth or a toothbrush

from the vet or pet shop. Toothbrushes made for dogs tend to have a longer handle and two heads, one at each end. They come in two sizes – for bigger or smaller mouths. I use a baby toothbrush. At the same time, pick up a tube of toothpaste specifically for dogs. It comes in all sorts of flavours – including chicken and beef. Dorwest make Roast Dinner toothpaste.

Warning

Don't ever use human toothpaste on your dog. Most human paste contains xylitol, a sweetener that is very toxic to dogs, and because you're not going to get him to rinse and spit, he's going to swallow it.

My advice is to start slowly, act casual. Whatever you do, don't give up. It's too important to neglect, and it's even worth working with a trainer if you can't get the hang of it. Some dogs won't ever get used to having their teeth cleaned. If your dog is one of these, at least start her on a daily seaweed supplement.

Start by putting some toothpaste on the cloth or brush, then gently rub it along the outer side of your dog's teeth and gums – there's no need to do the insides (unless he'll let you, then bravo). Your dog then takes over and spreads the toothpaste about by licking it. Job done in a minute or less.

My routine

This is how I got Nikita used to tooth cleaning.

Day one:

I got a tooth-cleaning cloth, a little sock for your finger, impregnated with colloidal silver, which kills bacteria. I put it on my finger and let Nikita get used to the smell, then I put a little chicken-flavoured toothpaste on it and let her lick it off.

Days two and three:

I did the same again, but this time I gently pushed my finger in between her gums and cheek and let her lick the toothpaste off while I gently rubbed a couple of teeth.

Days four and five:

Same again, but I moved my finger around the front and to the other side a little.

Day six:

This time I opened her mouth a little and brushed all her teeth, but didn't push right to the back.

Day seven:

I brushed all her teeth and have done ever since. I have worked out she prefers a baby toothbrush to the cloth finger!

CHAPTER 9

URINARY PROBLEMS

Dog urinary problems come in two sizes – minor and serious. If in any doubt, always consult a vet and treat an ongoing issue naturally only if anything serious has been ruled out. The advice that follows is suitable for urinary problems that are caused by old age, or ongoing issues that your vet has checked.

Urinary incontinence

Proper urinary incontinence is when your dog pees involuntarily, in small amounts, usually when she lies down. If your dog pees in the house – leaving a big puddle on the floor – it's far more likely to be a training issue or because she can't get outside to do it.

Urinary incontinence is much more common in older dogs, especially females and the larger, heavier breeds,and it's generally the result of hormone depletion. As dogs age, their oestrogen and testosterone levels fall and one of the side effects is that the muscles in the sphincter and the neck of the bladder become weaker, leading to leakage. Bad news for dogs – and us – but great news for pad manufacturers. Urinary incontinence can also be a result of spaying and neutering (hormones again), infections, kidney problems, spine and nerve damage and neurological conditions such as epilepsy.

Lying in pee is just as distressing for dogs as it would be for us. Not only that, but urine is caustic so can burn the skin if left on it for any length of time, which leads to soreness, pain and yet more distress. Signs of urinary incontinence include licking her bottom more than normal, wet fur on the back of her legs and/or generally smelling of pee.

Helping the bladder

The bladder and sphincter are essentially organs made of muscle, and just like the heart are there to make sure everything moves along smoothly. Think of them as traffic cops. All the waste is held back by the stern hand signal of the police officer until there is enough build-up of traffic and he has to let some through to ease congestion. Let's face it, though, once you've done that job for 50 years or so you're not as 'on it' as you used to be and things start to slide! Likewise, an older dog's muscles aren't as strong or as willing as they once were, which can lead to age-related incontinence.

The good news is there are a few well-tried and tested herbal and vegetable supplements available that work incredibly well – agrimony, raspberry leaf and mixed vegetable tablets. Agrimony is a member of the rose family and its use as a treatment for incontinence has been documented as far back as the Greeks and Romans. Its astringency is very effective for strengthening diminishing muscle tone in the sphincter. Add it to food daily to treat weakened bowel muscles. CSJ produce a herbal blend called Hold It! for dogs. It contains pure, chopped agrimony and the feedback on it is brilliant – it worked really well on our old Bedlington, BB, when she started having little accidents. Raspberry leaf tablets are more commonly used to tone the smooth muscle of the uterus before birth, but as the bladder also contains smooth muscle, dog owners are increasingly using it for incontinence and are reporting good results. Dorwest's are very good, as are their Mixed Vegetable tablets, which act as a mild diuretic, so your dog can empty her bladder fully, meaning less risk of leakage when she's asleep or lying down.

Relieving the external symptoms

As I've said, urine is caustic so can scald your dog's

skin, like nappy rash in a baby, and it's just as painful. Washing the affected areas with a flannel rinsed in a 4:1 solution of warm water and apple cider vinegar will really soothe and clean the skin. Pat the area dry and apply a soothing cream. I'd stay away from anything harsh and go for a coconut cream (not the edible stuff you add to a Thai curry) or Dermacton skin cream for dogs, which my customers rate highly. Avoid baby nappy cream as it will probably contain zinc, which can be toxic if ingested. Whatever you choose, make sure it doesn't contain steroids either. Stick to something nice and gentle made specifically for dogs. Rub it into clean skin a couple of times a day and it will really help. It will probably make you feel better, too, to know that at least you're offering relief for sore skin while you're working out what's causing the leaking.

Invest in washable bedding

Buy dog beds you can wash easily so your dog is not lying in urine. You can also line her bed with Vetbed or another good-quality, absorbent bedding that can be washed daily. I've known dog owners who've used small duvets with synthetic filling that can be washed easily – cot duvets are good.

CHAPTER 10

VACCINATIONS

To vaccinate or not to vaccinate is as emotive an issue for pet owners as it is for parents. So I'll get right off the fence with this one straight away – I think vaccines are the 20th century's gift to the world and that we should avail ourselves, our children and our pets of them at every opportunity. But I also believe that in the UK we over-vaccinate our pets and that needs to stop.

Risk v reality

It seems to me that these days everyone wants a cast-iron, 100 per cent guarantee that something will work all the time and won't ever fail; sadly, there is no such thing. Life doesn't come with any guarantees. We have to take a risk, based on our best guess and the information we have to hand. My view is that in the case of vaccines, the risk of not being vaccinated far outweighs the risk of any side effect we, or our pets, may suffer from having them. So we should roll up our sleeves, stick out our tongues and give thanks that we have access to them at all. That said, there's no need to overdo it. I get my pets vaccinated against core diseases and I also vaccinate myself against diseases when I am travelling. But I won't be vaccinating any of us on a regular basis just for the hell of it, or because the vet says I should.

How vaccines work

A vaccine introduces a weakened version of a disease (distemper, for instance) into the recipient (your dog). This triggers your dog's immune system to respond as if the body has been infected with the actual disease and it produces antibodies. If your dog then encounters the actual, much more powerful disease later on, the immune system recognises it and can immediately produce antibodies to fight it off, instead of going through the lengthy process of working out what it is first.

Core canine vaccines

A core vaccine is defined as one that all dogs, regardless of geographical location, should receive. Non-core vaccines are those required only by those animals whose location, environment or lifestyle puts them at risk of contracting a specific infection, for example rabies. In the UK dogs need the following core vaccines:

- Canine distemper virus (CDV)
- Canine adenovirus (CAV)
- Canine parvovirus type 2 (CPV-2)

When should dogs be vaccinated?

The vaccination guideline group (VGG) of the World Small Animal Veterinary Association (WSAVA) states:[1]

> The VGG recognises that maternally derived antibody (MDA) significantly interferes with the efficacy of most current core vaccines administered to puppies and kittens in early life. As the level of MDA varies significantly among litters, the VGG recommends the administration of three vaccine doses to pups and kittens, with the final dose of these being delivered at 14–16 weeks of age or above. In cultural or financial situations where a pet animal may only be permitted the benefit of a single vaccination, that vaccination should be with core vaccines at 16 weeks of age or above.

Your dog should then be given a booster at 12 months.

How long does a vaccine protect a dog?

The lifetime of a vaccine – the time for which it gives

1 1 http://www.wsava.org/sites/default/files/WSAVA%20Vaccination%20Guidelines%202015%20Full%20Version.pdf

complete or partial protection from a disease – is known as the duration of immunity, or DOI. Distemper vaccine, for example, provides a DOI of nine years or longer – whereas if your dog contracted distemper 'naturally' and survived he would develop a lifelong DOI.

In general, the duration of immunity is many years, and often much longer than many vaccination manufacturers suggest. See page 136 for how often to vaccinate.

What would one of these diseases do to my dog?

It depends on the disease, of course, but consider this before you dismiss vaccination out of hand: how ill a dog becomes and his survival depends on his general health. A dog with a compromised immune system, who can't be vaccinated, will not only be at a high risk of contracting infections, but will also not be able to fight the disease as easily. A high take-up of vaccinations among dog owners means that a herd immunity is created, which protects the dogs that cannot be immunised. But, if you really need to know – check out canine distemper, in the box opposite.

Canine distemper – a horrible way to go

Of all infectious diseases, this is the one that causes the most deaths in dogs worldwide. It's a bit like the measles virus in humans and is 'shed' from infected animals through all their secretions, including tears.

The distemper virus attacks the cells that line the surfaces of the dog's body and organs, including the brain. The symptoms start off with fever, move on to listlessness, discharge from eyes and nose and loss of appetite. The dog will also suffer from vomiting and diarrhoea, which leads to dehydration. After a while the discharge from the nose becomes thick and sticky. Your dog starts to cough and pus blisters appear on his abdomen. As if all this wasn't bad enough, the virus then gets stuck into the brain, causing encephalitis (inflammation of the lining of the brain). Your dog starts to slobber, shakes his head repeatedly and starts chewing at nothing (remember the poor, mad cows?). On it goes, ending with seizures, and possibly death.

Now, when was the last time you saw a dog doing that? I'm guessing, if you don't work in a veterinary surgery, probably never. And why would you want to? It's a horrible way to go and it takes weeks. You haven't seen it because we vaccinate against it.

Puppies and maternal immunity

Puppies, like human babies, are born with a maternal immunity from maternally derived antibodies (MDA), also known as passive immunity. Maternal antibodies interfere with vaccination efficacy in the early weeks, which is why puppies don't have their first vaccination until they are eight to nine weeks old. They then receive a second vaccination two weeks later. These vaccinations essentially act as a trigger for your puppy's body to develop an immune response of its own.

It's then recommended that dogs receive a booster at 12 months. This helps to ensure immunity in dogs who didn't respond so well to the first set of vaccines because their maternal immunity hadn't worn off sufficiently.

Older and immune-compromised dogs and pregnant bitches

Dogs in these groups should be vaccinated under the supervision of your vet. Nikita, for instance, won't be having any more vaccinations, at the recommendation of the vets who rescued her.

Annual boosters? I don't think so

This is where I hop over to the other side of the fence. For years it's been standard practice for all dogs and cats to be revaccinated with annual booster jabs. The WSAVA's 2015 vaccination guidelines advise against this practice. In summary, the organisation states that:

- Vaccines should not be given needlessly
- Core vaccines should not be given more frequently than every three years after the 12-month booster injection that follows the puppy/kitten series, because the DOI is many years and may be up to the lifetime of the pet
- Only give core vaccines and vaccinate less frequently

However, my first question would be – if the DOI is nine years for the core diseases, why is it recommended that we revaccinate our dogs every three? I don't think it's the vets' fault. Look at their dilemma. The manufacturer will advise how often their vaccines should be administered so your dog remains protected. If a manufacturer stipulates every three years what's a vet to do? Even if she knows your dog and the local area well, the manufacturer has stated a limited time period in which they guarantee protection.

Would you take the risk of extending that time period with someone else's pet? I wouldn't. If the vet doesn't vaccinate your dog every three years and your dog goes on to develop one of these diseases, who're you going to blame (or sue)? And what if your doggy day care or kennels won't accept your dog unless he's fully vaccinated? There goes your two-week holiday.

Also, the veterinary world is changing. Practices are becoming far more business savvy, and many are now owned by very big companies. Some of these companies are in turn owned by very hungry shareholders who want their slice of the 'parvo' pie at the end of the year. So sales targets (yes, damned sales targets) are becoming more of an issue now. If a vet's practice vaccinates dogs every three years instead of every nine and they get 100 dogs a week sloping into the surgery, you get the business sense.

I return to the WSAVA's guidelines: 'The VGG strongly supports the concept of the "annual health check" which removes the emphasis from, and client expectation of, annual revaccination. The annual health check may still encompass administration of selected non-core vaccines, which should be administered annually, as the DOI for these products is generally one year or less.' If your vet or insurance company insists you have annual core vaccine boosters, get a new vet and/or change your insurance provider.

Alternatives to vaccination

The British Association of Homeopathic Veterinary

Surgeons (BAHVS) – a group of vets who are qualified in both conventional veterinary medicine and homeopathy – state: 'Where there is no medical contraindication, immunisation should be carried out in the normal way using the conventional tested and approved vaccines.'

Don't not vaccinate in the first place. There is no clinically proven alternative to a primary course of vaccinations. But after the initial vaccinations and first booster it's possible to test for antibodies (a titre test, see page 141) to establish if further vaccination is needed. If not, then great; carry on as normal.

Homeopathy

At the risk of upsetting and offending homeopaths, and some of my own lovely customers, homeopathic vaccines are a myth and in no way a safe substitute for a pharmaceutical live vaccine. Homeopathic vaccines, known as nosodes, are supposed to work in the same way that a vaccine does. However, a vaccine works by taking some of the live virus, distemper, for instance, and introducing it to the body, which produces antibodies to fight it off. A nosode, on the other hand, works by taking a tiny amount of a disease from diseased tissue – secretions, excretions or discharges – diluting it down to something so small that it is often undetectable, and then administering it to the patient's body, where it supposedly triggers an immune response to produce antibodies and fight the infection. The problem is, this is not a regulated industry so you have no way of knowing if the material was safe, if it was infected with any other diseased material and what effect it will have on the body once introduced.

Time and again I hear people say that they have given their dog nosodes instead of vaccines and he's been fine. I say, it's not the nosodes, you're just so, so lucky your dog hasn't been exposed to any of the core diseases. Vaccines have almost wiped out some horrific diseases in humans and animals so that we have forgotten how horrible, debilitating and lethal they can be. If homeopathy was so good as a method of immunising us and our pets, we would have been doing it for a long time before vaccines came along.

My only advice to you is that if you are still considering using nosodes as an alternative to vaccination for your pet, please get the core vaccines done first and then see a homeopathic vet for follow-ups. Don't buy nosodes off the internet, and ask your homeopathic vet who makes up their preparations, assuming they don't do it themselves.

So, to vaccinate or not to vaccinate?

Whatever your beliefs around your own health, not vaccinating your pet at all is really not an option. At the very least your pet needs his first round of vaccines. If money is very tight, just get the vaccinations done when your puppy is 16 weeks old, when it shouldn't clash with any passive immunity he will have inherited from his mother. If money is the issue, there are schemes out there to help with the cost. Look on the Dogs Trust, PDSA, Blue Cross and RSPCA websites for details. Also look out for National Vaccination Month. Each year there is a vaccination amnesty when vets across the country offer good discounts on core vaccines. Go to www.nvmonline.co.uk.

If you look at the Veterinary Medicines Directorate's report on Suspected Adverse Events for 2012 you will see that only 259 adverse reactions to live vaccines in dogs were reported. Which perhaps sounds like a lot. But when you consider how many dogs are vaccinated in any one year, it's negligible. Also, compare it to the horrible suffering and loss of life you would be facing if you didn't vaccinate and your dog contracted a deadly disease.

Titre testing

Before your dog's three-year booster is due, you may want to get a titre test done to determine whether or not she needs vaccinating. A titre test measures antibody levels in the dog's system – and thereby the level of immunity to a disease. Did you ever have a BCG (TB) vaccination at school when you were in your early teens? Do you remember everyone lining up a couple of weeks beforehand to have a little daisy wheel of something shot into your arm? That was a titre test and it was measuring your immunity to TB. If you had good immunity you didn't need the BCG vaccination. Once again, back to the WSAVA's view: 'The VGG supports the development and use of simple in-practice tests for determination of seroconversion (antibody) following vaccination.' This is a massive position shift for veterinary guidelines and it's about time. I think titre testing is going to become the norm in the next 10 years or so. And if vets can offer it as a service, still get your dog in for her health check and pay the rent then everyone's a winner.

Ask your vet about titre testing

More and more vets are starting to offer titre testing – my vet, for instance, charges £70 to do it. Simple titre tests, for distemper and parvo antibodies, can be carried out while you wait, if your vet's practice is set up to do them. Otherwise they have to go off to the lab to be checked. For rabies it's probably going to have to be sent off, and will cost more. But if you're not in a rabies area and you don't intend to travel to one with your dog, it's not something you need to worry about.

Thanks for reading

So you've read the book and now you're hatching a plan to tackle your dog's heinously smelly breath. Hooray! My work here is done.

Remember to step back and take an overall view of your dog, refer to the book whenever you need to, and breathe. Over time you will build up your bespoke medicine chest of goodies and use it to maintain your dog's health, and to sort out any niggling issues, as and when they crop up.

You will be a saint-style dog owner. Actually you already are.

KATE BENDIX worked for many years in television documentaries, before setting up her website, www.myitchydog.co.uk. She is an experienced broadcaster and features regularly on radio shows discussing dog health. Her previous books include *Top Dog* and *The Dog Diet* (Short Books).